Workbook for American Politics

Lydia Andrade

University of the Incarnate Word

and

Scott Dittloff

University of the Incarnate Word

Kendall Hunt
publishing company

www.kendallhunt.com
Send all inquiries to:
4050 Westmark Drive
Dubuque, IA 52004-1840

Printed in the United States of America
10 9 8 7 6 5 4 3 2

Dedication

This book is dedicated to the friends and colleagues who have advised us and counseled us over the years and to the students who have taught us how to be great teachers. Their enthusiasm and willingness to share their experiences and expertise have helped mold and refine our teaching. Our success in teaching is in no small measure the result of the mentoring of them all.

Table of Contents

Preface

We have designed this book as a study resource for students who are taking an introductory American politics course. The book addresses not only how to study, but how to read a textbook strategically. Other than the introduction, each chapter covers one topic that is typically covered in an American politics textbook. We start out by identifying what we consider to be some of the most important concepts related to that topic and then provide a list of key terms with definitions. We have also included exercises that are designed to be completed and turned in to the instructor. These exercises are designed to help the students engage the material and thus understand it better and to also help instructors get a feel for how well students understand the material. By recognizing where students are understanding course materials and where they are not, both students and instructors can take action to help students learn better and get better grades.

This book works best in conjunction with a basic American politics textbook and should not be used in place of a textbook. It is designed to help students get more out of both course reading assignments as well as in-class lectures and activities. We recommend that you complete the course reading and the corresponding workbook assignments either before you cover a specific topic in class or at the same time you are covering the topic in class. You will be engaging in several different kinds of learning and should increase not only your comprehension but your retention of the material (which should mean a better grade!).

Introduction

Why We Wrote This Book

We have taught this class for much longer than we would care to admit. While trends and students come and go, one constant remains: many students are uncertain how to be successful in their academic pursuits. While they may have a basic store of information, they are uncertain how to manage that information and how to build on it. Thus we often see students who are shocked they did so poorly on their first American politics exam. When they come to see us about how they can improve their grades, we quickly find out that in many cases the student cannot distinguish between important and unimportant material. They either have too much information to remember or not enough to answer test questions adequately.

The problem for students is usually not that the material is too difficult; it is that they do not know how to study properly. So, we spend our time talking to students about how to take notes, how to study, how to prepare for class: in short, we work with them on how to be a student. After years of having these discussions with students, we decided to create this workbook to help students practice isolating the key concepts and developing a *thorough* understanding of the material.

Purpose of These Exercises

The exercises in this workbook are not designed to replace class time or time spent reading your book. They are designed to help students recognize what is important (at least in part) and how to make sense of it. That means you should plan on doing all the exercises in the chapters – even if the professor has not assigned them as homework. It also means that you should do this work ahead of time. Do not wait until the last minute. Think of this as practice or study time for the test. If you do it ahead of time you will be well prepared and have a much better sense of what is in the chapters, what you "have to know" and what material is more challenging for you (that means the stuff you should get help with!).

There are four sections in each chapter and each should help you study in a slightly different way. The Concepts section identifies the main ideas in the chapter. Think of these as possible essay questions which you have to explain. So if you look at a concept and have no idea what it is or how to explain it—you should go back to the chapter and re-read that section. It also means that if you recognize the concept but cannot give more than a 1 sentence explanation you are also NOT ready. You should be able to EXPLAIN these ideas.

The Key Terms section of the chapters simply identifies the political science/government terms used in the chapter. You should review them and make sure you know them but do NOT assume simply recognizing the definition will be enough. These will rarely be used as questions on the exam. You are expected to know them and use them in answering essay questions. They are basics you are expected to master.

The Exercises are intended to let you put your knowledge to use. You will find most of these questions are not fill in the blank or essays in which all you have to do is look up the answer in the text. These questions are application based. So you have to take what you have learned and read and apply it to real life. These questions may take you a bit longer to answer but if you take them seriously they should help you develop a richer understanding of the material. A deeper understanding will help you do a better job answering questions on exams.

The Multiple Choice questions are designed to review the basic concepts of the chapter and give you some practice recognizing how the material might be presented on a quiz. You should use these exercises as a test for yourself. If you find you have to look up the answer or debate about the proper answer – then you are not ready for the exam!

How to Prepare for the Exam

Cramming for a test is not good. Last minute, marathon sessions of studying (often late into the night before an exam) are inefficient, ineffective, time-consuming, and waste time because you have to spend a lot of time trying to remember concepts that you probably have not given much thought to. The recall of facts, ideas, and concepts requires that you read and re-read material. If you have to cram right before the test, you are not only having to comprehend but you are trying to memorize as well. Memorization takes time. You will have to spend time simply going over material to see it enough times to remember it.

Cramming also means you are probably studying at the last minute. This is generally too late to determine if you have understood the material. It is also too late to determine if you have focused on the correct material.

This book is designed to help make your studying more efficient and effective by making you spend time with material over weeks instead of over hours. You may spend the same amount of time in the end, but you will do it when you are better prepared to remember. It will also ask you to address whether you actually understand the material. The better you understand the material, the better you will do on the test. The material will make more sense and will be easier to remember if you have given yourself time enough to learn it. Moreover, if you read, review, and do these exercises in the weeks prior to the test, you will know long before the test, if you understand the material or not. This is important—if you find that you are having trouble with the material and you have waited until the night before the exam to study there is little chance you will be able to figure it out or get help in time.

Notes

Probably the most important thing you can do to ensure your success in this class is to take good notes and get notes when you miss class. Simply writing down the PowerPoint bullet points will not work! You need to write down the main points of the lecture as well as the evidence and explanations used to support it. Remember, your notes are intended to help YOU learn and recall the information. So make sure you write down the ideas and explanations in your own words. Write down *all* the information you are going to need to remember for the test. Most people learn and remember material from their notes better than from the book – so make sure you get all the necessary notes and you get them correctly.

Make sure your notes are good by (at least once) going over them with your professor to see if what you wrote down as the main points agrees with what the professor thinks are the most important points. If you discover your notes are not as comprehensive or thorough as they need to be, discuss with your professor exactly what is missing. Use a specific day's notes and go over what you wrote down and what the Professor thinks you missed. Then in the next class period make a concerted effort to be more thorough in your note taking—then have the Professor look them over one more time. Chances are your notes will have improved significantly.

Once you are comfortable that your notes are good, it is time to turn your attention to learning them. In order to do well you need to MEMORIZE your notes. Memorize means that you can close your notebook or computer and you can say—out loud—what is on the page. If you don't close the notebook—you will cheat. You will sneak a look at the page to remind yourself. But if it is closed and you have to recite it out loud, you will hear when you know it and when you are stumbling. Make sure you read your notes over two to three times a week as the semester progresses. You will find that as you revisit them again and again, your studying time will be more efficient. You will read the notes faster because you will recognize and begin to remember the material. By the time the exam arrives, you will not have to spend hours right before the test learning and trying to remember what you have not looked at for days or weeks. PLUS it gives you the opportunity to get help and/or additional explanation of any material in your notes. Anything that you have in your notes which isn't clear to you when review it—you should ask your professor about.

Book

Reading the book and determining what material will be required for the test is one of the most difficult tasks for most students. But if you approach your reading strategically, you should be able to read efficiently and effectively. First, determine if you are someone who does better by reading before a topic is discussed in class or after (and what the professor prefers you to do). Read in the way which best suits YOUR learning style.

DO NOT get behind in the reading. If you are still reading the night before the test you are probably in trouble. It is not possible to do all the reading and learn all that is needed the night before the exam.

The first thing you should do upon starting a new chapter is to make a BRIEF outline before reading. This just means you should jot down all the headings and sub-headings of the chapter (use the font style, color, etc. to determine the structure of the outline). Use this as a reference when you are reading. It may help with that feeling of "I understand what I just read but I don't know why the authors made me read it" or "What was the point of that?" By having the chapter outlines as a reference you can always look back and see why the authors were talking about some point for several pages—you should be able to see how it fits in the body of the rest of the chapter. It will give you context. The following example is what the title and subject headings of a chapter on federalism might include.

Federalism
Constitutional Basis for Federalism
Horizontal Federalism
National Constitutional Supremacy
     Milestones in National Government Supremacy
Disputes over Division of Power
     Dual federalism
     Cooperative federalism
     New Federalism
Fiscal Federalism
     Grants-in-Aid
          Categorical grants
          Project grants
          Block grants
          Revenue Sharing
Overloaded Federalism
State and Local Governmental Costs Demanded by the Federal Government
     Unfunded Mandates

So, if you find yourself reading about block grants and saying "why are they telling me this?" you can look at your outline. Block grants are a part of fiscal federalism and federalism is about the distribution of power between levels of government – THAT is why it was in the chapter.

Your textbook is not a novel. You should approach it with the question in mind: "what do I need here? What is the point they are trying to explain?" Read your textbook deliberately. By that, we mean use the title and subject headings of the text as indicators of what is important in that section of the book. The headings are the authors' way of telling you what the point of each section is. So you should use them as a sign of what you need to learn or take away from each part of the book.

You cannot effectively read a chapter all at one time! Look at the sections of the chapters as individual lectures—you do not hear all the lectures on a given topic in a single day so why do you think you can read them all in one sitting? Space out your reading—do a bit each day. And if you are going to read part of a chapter, be deliberate in where you start and end. Use the chapter headings as indicators of topics and sub-topics and read the full section. Don't stop in the middle of a section as that will make it more difficult to remember the points of that section.

Make notes in the margins when material is difficult. If you read something and it makes sense but is complex then write a note to yourself in the margins explaining that

4

material in your words. You are the one who is going to read/ review those notes later so make it easy for yourself. For example, assume that the following text on the left is from your textbook. The comments on the right are notes to help you quickly find and learn the important points. The underlining and numbering at various points highlight in the text the notes you have taken in the margin.

Textbook passage example	Margin notes examples
Common law is the <u>British system of judge-made law that has slowly developed over centuries. It is a system of law based on precedent</u> that requires judges to make their decisions based on principles that judges previously made in similar cases.	Common law definition = British system of law based on the decisions in previous cases
The history of common law stretches back to the time of the Norman Conquest. The new rulers worked to establish central governmental administration as well as courts of law (Neubauer 1997:26). At first, laws were local and justice was administered locally. However, a distinctly national body of law began to develop as the local jurisdiction began to be replaced by national or royal law. William the Conqueror had created a royal court to protect monarchical interests as well as to act as a court of appeals. King William as well as subsequent monarchs, being busy with ruling the kingdom, did not have the time or inclination to hear appeals of controversies among the subjects. Monarchs enlisted the assistance of "royal officials," the Privy Court, to decide private controversies. <u>These officials based their decisions on the "common" customs of the kingdom rather than on local custom or culture. This is how the term "common law" was born.</u>	History of common law Norman Conquest William the Conqueror Privy Court Origin of the term common law = legal decisions were based on the "common" customs of the kingdom

The idea is not to rewrite the book in the margins. The objective is to highlight the important points and to provide a brief description in your own words that you can view quickly. By putting the notes next to the passage in the text where the author describes the point, if you forget or do not understand the point, you can simply look across to the text for a fuller explanation.

Make notes in the margins tying things together. So if the author is describing "5 factors that influence…" make sure you put a big "1", "2", etc. out in the margin next to where that point is discussed and in the text. See the example below. Often these descriptions can take pages and pages so this will help you remember when reviewing that this is part of a larger list and what those main points are.

Textbook Passage Example	Margin Notes Example

There are three historical reasons for federalism in the United States: common problems shared by each state^1; large geographical size of many states with limited population combined with isolation of large segments of the population^2; and sectionalism and political subcultures which led many to advocate a pluralistic form of government^3.
 	
Current arguments for federalism tend to focus on two major areas: the ability to unite a large population^1 while still allowing the people to have control over local problems^2. Arguments against federalism in the United States are usually seen as unpatriotic.
	3 arguments for choosing federalism
	   1 large size of states
	
	  2 isolation of the populace
	
	  3 different political cultures
	
	2 current arguments for federalism
	   1. Unite a large population
	
	   2. Give people control over local issues
	
	Arguments against federalism=unpatriotic

Finally, if you read something in the book which you do not understand (or you understand what they are talking about but you are not sure what you are supposed to do with it), contact your professor. Stop by. Send an email. Get clarification!

Test

There are some simple test taking strategies which may make a big difference in your final grade.

Before you start writing, take a look at the test and determine which questions you *have* to answer and, if there are choices, which you *want* to answer. Make sure you know what you are being asked to do on the exam. And if questions do not make sense to you – ask for clarification!

Make a BRIEF outline for each essay or short answer question before starting to write ANY of your answers. This just means you should jot down all the headings and sub-headings of the points you want to address in your answer. This will help you in three ways: First, you won't forget points you want to address. Once you start writing answers to other

6

questions, you will be so focused on other things that you may well forget what you want to write in your answers for questions that you get to later on during the test. If you write an outline down first, you'll have the points there to remind you. Second, you can organize your answer. Rather than discussing your points in whatever random order they popped into your mind, you can reorder your outline points to create the most logical order for your answer. Finally, if you tend to get stressed during tests, jotting down the points you want to make will help reassure you that you know what it is that you want to say and that you are ready!

For example, if you were asked to answer an essay question about the purpose/function of constitutions, you might have a list like the following:

What do Constitutions do?
- Establish the structure of government
- Set the fundamental rules of the game of politics
- Tell the government what it can and cannot do
- Tell the people what they can and cannot do.

It is not necessary that the points be in any particular order when you initially jot them down because you can easily rearrange them by putting numbers on them and then write your essay accordingly. So if you wanted to address the importance of civil liberties first, you could simply renumber them as in the example below.

3) Establish the structure of government
4) Prescribe the fundamental rules of the game of politics
1) Tell the government what it can and cannot do
2) Tell the people what they can and cannot do.

You also do not have to add any more detail to your list as this is just a tool to help remind you of what you want to say. If you are prepared for the test, the entire process of writing down your answer outline should not take more than a couple of minutes, so do not worry about losing time doing this. This will help you write more efficiently and effectively, so you will more than make up for the small expenditure of time.

Last But Not Least

TALK TO YOUR PROFESSOR BEFORE YOU ARE IN TROUBLE! GET HELP WHEN YOU NEED IT! Remember, this is your class and your grade. So if you need help or want to discuss the material you should not be shy about going and speaking with your professor. Really, that is what they pay us for!

GOOD LUCK!

Dr. Lydia Andrade and Dr. Scott Dittloff

Workbook Chapter 1 – Federalism

Concepts

Concurrent Powers

Cooperative Federalism

Dual Federalism

Enumerated Powers

Grants in Aid

Horizontal Federalism

Implied Powers

New Federalism

Shared Powers

Key Terms

Block Grant—A type of federal grant which provides funds for a general policy area but provides state and local governments discretion in designing the specific programs.

Categorical Grant—A type of federal grant that provides money for a specific policy activity and details how the programs are to be carried out.

Concurrent Powers—The powers listed in the Constitution as belonging to both the national and state governments.

Confederation—A political system in which the central government receives no direct grant of power from the people and can only exercise the power granted to it by the regional governments.

Cooperative Federalism—The idea that the distinction between state and national responsibilities is unclear and that the different levels of government share responsibilities in many areas.

Crossover Sanctions—Conditions placed on grant money, which have nothing to do with the original purpose of the grant.

Cyclical Federalism—The idea that the national government takes on a greater policy role during liberal periods of U.S. history and less so in conservative periods.

Devolution—The returning of policy power and responsibility to the states from the national government.

Dual Federalism—The idea that the national and state governments are sovereign, with separate and distinct jurisdictions.

Enabling Act—A provision in a law that confers the power to implement or enforce the law. For example, a resolution passed by Congress authorizing residents of a territory to draft a state constitution is part of the process of adding new states to the Union.
Enumerated Powers—The powers specifically listed in the Constitution as belonging to the national government.

Federalism—A political system in which regional governments share power with the national government.

Full Faith and Credit—The provision in the Constitution which requires states to honor the civil obligations (wills, marriages, etc.) generated by other states.

General Revenue Sharing—A type of federal grant that returns money to the state and local governments with no requirements as to how it is spent.

Grants-in-aid—A form of national subsidy to the states designed to help and encourage policy initiatives.

Home Rule—The power of local governments to make some of their own laws/regulations without having to obtain prior approval of the state or national governments.
Interstate Rendition—The obligation of states to return persons accused of a crime to the state from which they fled.

Implied Powers—Those powers belonging to the national government that are suggested in the Constitution's "necessary and proper" clause.

New Federalism—A movement to take power away from the federal government and return it to the states.

Nullification—The act of declaring a national law null and void within a state's borders.

Police Power—The authority of the states to pass laws for the health, safety, and morals of their citizens.

Plebiscite—A direct vote of all eligible voters on a policy related question.
Preemption—Congress expressly giving national laws precedence over state and local laws.

Republican Government—A form of government in which the government operates with the consent of the governed through some type of representative institution.

Supreme Law of the Land—The idea that the laws passed by Congress and the treaties made by the federal government are supreme and state constitutions and laws are subordinate to them.

Unitary—A political system in which the power is concentrated in the national government and the regional governments can only exercise those powers granted them by the central government.

Application

1. In your own words, explain the advantages and disadvantages of a federal system.

2. Think of 10 examples of how government influences our daily lives (Ex: speed limits, airline security). Which level of government is doing this activity (federal, state, local).

	Government Activity	Level of Government
1.		
2.		
3.		
4.		
5.		
6.		
7.		
8.		
9.		
10.		

Explain how all these reflect the ideas of federalism.

3. Explain the role of government funding and grants in federalism.

4. Read Federalist #51. In your own words explain how Madison believes power should be distributed between the national and state governments. Why does he argue this?

5. Go to the URL: http://www.cas.sc.edu/poli/courses/scgov/History_of_Federalism.htm and in your own words identify and define the different types of federalism. Which model is a more accurate representation of the federal/state relationship? Create your own metaphor for each of the types of federalism.

6. Go to the URL
   http://www.nga.org/portal/site/nga/menuitem.67948e4cf7b28b7ae8ebb856a11010a0/, and
   click on the link for No Child Left Behind. Does this reflect Dual Federalism or
   Cooperative Federalism? Why? How?

7. Go to the URL http://www.csg.org/policy/fed/default.aspx Does this reflect Dual
   Federalism or Cooperative Federalism? Why? How?

Multiple Choice Questions

1. A political system in which regional governments share power with the national government is called a _____ system.

   a. confederate
   b. unitary
   c. federal
   d. none of the above

2. A political system in which the central government receives only those powers that the regional governments choose to give it is called a _____ system.
   a. confederate
   b. unitary
   c. federal
   d. none of the above

3. The _____ powers are those specifically listed in the Constitution as belonging to the national government.
   a. implied
   b. concurrent
   c. reserved
   d. enumerated

4. The power of the states to pass laws concerning the morals of their citizens is known as the _____ powers.
   a. concurrent
   b. police
   c. reserved
   d. none of the above

5. Which of the following is NOT part of the process of adding a new state to the Union?
   a. Congress passes an enabling act
   b. Congress forms an incorporated territory
   c. All state legislatures approve the admission of the new state
   d. Residents of the territory petition Congress

6. The idea that state laws and constitutions are subordinate to the national constitution is known as_____.
   a. "full faith and credit"
   b. "supreme law of the land"
   c. "devolution"
   d. none of the above

7. The returning of power to the states from the national government is called
   _____.
   - a. federalism
   - b. cooperative federalism
   - c. devolution
   - d. dual federalism

8. Which of the following influenced the evolution of federalism?
   - a. The buildup for World War II
   - b. The New Deal
   - c. World War I
   - d. All of the above

9. The idea that national and state governments are sovereign with separate and distinct jurisdiction is known as _____.
   - a. cooperative federalism
   - b. new federalism
   - c. devolution
   - d. dual federalism

10. A grant program in which money is given to the states and local governments to spend as they wish is known as _____.
    - a. general revenue sharing
    - b. block grants
    - c. categorical grants
    - d. none of the above

11. A grant program in which money is given to the state and local governments for specific programs and specifies how the programs should be carried out is known as
    _____.
    - a. general revenue sharing
    - b. block grants
    - c. categorical grants
    - d. none of the above

12. Requirements and conditions placed on federal grants that have nothing to do with the original purpose of the grant are known as _____.
    - a. spending restrictions
    - b. crossover sanctions
    - c. categorical restrictions
    - d. federal requirements

13. The program first introduced by President Nixon that sought to reverse the expansion of the federal government was called _____.
    a. dual federalism
    b. cooperative federalism
    c. new federalism
    d. state-centered federalism

14. The idea that Congress can pass a law expressly giving national law precedence over some state or local law is known as _____.
    a. supreme power
    b. preemption
    c. legislative supremacy
    d. none of the above

15. Which of the following court decisions helped foster New Federalism?
    a. Printz v. United States
    b. New York v. United States
    c. Kimmel v. Florida Board of Regents
    d. All of the above

16. The idea that the national government takes on a greater policy role during liberal periods of US history and less of a role in conservative periods is known as _____.
    a. ideological federalism
    b. new federalism
    c. cyclical federalism
    d. none of the above

17. A federal system reflects a conflict between the basic democratic values of:
    a. equality and freedom
    b. liberty and freedom
    c. liberty and equality
    d. equality and justice

18. The advantages of federalism, as seen by the framers of the Constitution, include:
    a. it is a way to accommodate the diverse interests of a large nation
    b. it disperses power
    c. it facilitates variation in public policy
    d. all of the above

19. The disadvantages of federalism include all of the following EXCEPT:
    a. it may make it hard for citizens to hold government accountable
    b. there is the potential for national government to become too powerful
    c. states may become too powerful
    d. it facilitates variation in public policy

20. The ability of the national government to increase their power through the doctrine of implied powers was first tested in:
    a. McCulloch v. Maryland
    b. Brown v. Board of Education
    c. New York v. United States
    d. Kimmel v. Florida Board of Regents

Workbook Chapter 2 – Constitution and Founding

Concepts

Anti-Federalist

Articles of Confederation

Autocracy

Constitution

Democracy

Direct Democracy

Equality

Federalist

Formal Amendment

Informal Amendment

Liberty

Madisonian Dilemma

Oligarchy

Representative Democracy

Key Terms

Absolute Majority—Often referring to elections, it means obtaining fifty percent plus one of the total vote.

Anti-federalists—The group of people who opposed a stronger national government than existed under the Articles of Confederation and opposed the ratification of the Constitution.

Articles of Confederation—An agreement among the thirteen original states that provided a loose national government. There was no direct grant of power to the national government from the people and it could only exercise the power granted to it by the thirteen states.

Autocracy—A form of government in which the power to make authoritative decisions and allocate resources is vested in one person.

Bicameral—A legislature with two chambers.

Check and Balance—The idea that each branch of the federal government should assert and protect its own rights but must also cooperate with the other branches. Each branch is to serve as a limit on the other's powers, balancing the overall distribution of power.

Civil Liberties—Protections given to individuals against arbitrary governmental actions.

Connecticut Compromise—A proposal at the Constitutional Convention that called for a two-house legislature with a House of Representatives apportioned on the basis of population and a Senate representing each state on an equal basis.

Constituency—The group of people served by an elected official or branch of government.

Constitution—A document that provides the basic principles that determine the conduct of political affairs.

Constitutionalism—The idea of limited government that cannot deny the fundamental rights of the people.

Custom and Usage—The term used to describe Constitutional change which occurs when the practices and institutions of government not specifically mentioned in the Constitution change over time through use and evolution.

Democracy—A form of government in which all the citizens have the opportunity to participate in the process of making authoritative decisions and allocating resources.

Economic Equality—The idea that each individual receives the same amount of material goods, regardless of his/her contribution to society.

Elitist—A term used to describe a society in which organized, influential minority interests dominate the political process.

Employment Act of 1946—A law that dramatically increased the role of the federal government in promoting economic prosperity and full employment.

Enumerated Powers—The powers specifically listed in the Constitution.

Equality of Opportunity—The idea that every individual has the right to develop to the fullest extent of his/her abilities.

Equality under the Law—The idea that the law is supposed to be applied impartially, without regard for the identity or status of the individual involved.

Executive Privilege—A prerogative power of the President to withhold information on matters of national security or personal privacy.

Federalism—The division of power between the national and state governments that attempts to balance power by giving each separate powers as well as the ability to check the other.

Federalist—The group of people comprised primarily of professional classes and soldiers who sought change and a stronger national government than existed under the Articles of Confederation. They supported the adoption of the Constitution.

Federalist Papers—A series of political essays published to persuade New Yorkers to ratify the Constitution. Today they provide the best source for understanding the rationale and justification for the Constitution.

Government—Individuals, institutions, and processes that make the rules for society and possess the power to enforce them.

Implied Powers—The powers not formally specified in the Constitution , but rather are suggested or implied by those that are listed.

Initiative—An election in which voters are asked to make policy decisions.

Interest Group—A group organized around a set of views or preferences in order to try and influence government decision makers.

Judicial Review—The power of the courts to determine the constitutionality of acts of the legislative and executive branches.

Limited Government—a government whose functions and powers are prescribed and limited by law.

Madisonian Dilemma—The problem of balancing individual liberty and the freedoms that make it possible.

Mixed Government—The idea that government should represent both property and people.

New Jersey Plan—A proposal presented at the Constitutional Convention that called for a one-house legislature with equal representation for each state.

Oligarchy—A form of government in which the power to make authoritative decisions and allocate resources is vested in a small group of people.

Pluralist—A society in which the power is widely distributed among diverse groups and interests.

Plurality—When there are more than two candidates, the person who receives the most votes receives a plurality of votes even though this person may have less than a majority.

Political Party—A group of persons organized primarily for the purpose of controlling government through winning elections and holding public office.

Politics—The process of making decisions and coming to some agreement about "who gets what."

Popular Sovereignty—The idea that the highest political authority in a democracy is the will of the people.

Prerogative or Inherent Powers—These powers are not listed or implied by the Constitution but rather have been claimed as essential to the national government.

Reciprocity—The state of mutual dependence and influence that describes the relationship between office holders and the general populace.

Representative Democracy—A system of government in which ordinary citizens choose public officials to represent and make decisions for them.

Republican Government—A form of government in which the people elect representatives to make the decisions of governing.

Right of Privacy—being free from intrusion in the private life or affairs of citizens. The Constitutional right of privacy has developed alongside a statutory right of privacy which limits access to personal information.

Separation of Powers—The idea that each branch of government is authorized to carry out a separate part of the political process.

Social Security Act of 1935—A law that greatly expanded the role of the federal government in basic welfare services.

Sovereignty—Exclusive right to exercise supreme political authority over a geographic region and the people residing therein.

Theory—An abstraction that focuses on the essential elements of complex real-world phenomena.

Virginia Plan—The first major proposal presented at the 1787 Constitutional Convention. This was the basis of the Constitution.

Application

1. List the advantages and disadvantages of democracy as opposed to autocracy or oligarchy.

2. In your own words, explain the difference between direct and representative democracy.

   Which would you prefer if it were up to you to choose? Why?

3. Explain the idea of majority rule vs. minority rights. List 3 current political issues which demonstrate this tension. Explain your answers.

    1.

    2.

    3.

4. In your own words, explain the purpose of a constitution. Explain the basic components or aspects of governing which would be covered in a Constitution. Provide an example of each.

5. In your own words, explain the positions of the Federalists and Anti-federalists.

6. In your own words explain the Madisonian dilemma. List examples from the current political environment which demonstrates this.

7. Explain how the meaning of the U.S. Constitution can be changed over time – other than through the formal amendment process.

8. Go to the URL: http://www.barefootsworld.net/aoc1777.html and in your own words, briefly describe the powers of the state and national governments under the Articles of Confederation. Why did the Articles of Confederation fail?

9. Go to the URL: http://www.usconstitution.net/consttop_fedr.html and identify and describe the different types of governmental systems. Why did the United States choose to adopt the governmental system it did?

10. Using the same website as in #9, Identify and define the types of powers granted to the national and state governments.

What types of powers are granted to the national government? Give examples.

What types of powers are granted to the state governments? Give examples.

What powers are denied to government? Give examples.

Multiple Choice Questions

1. A form of government in which the power to make decisions and allocate resources is given to a small group of people is called:

   a. autocracy
   b. representative democracy
   c. oligarchy
   d. authoritarianism

2. The idea that the highest political authority should come from the will of the people is referred to as:
   a. equality under the law
   b. popular sovereignty
   c. social equality
   d. none of the above

3. The idea that people should be free of class or social barriers and discrimination is called _____.
   a. equality under the law
   b. economic equality
   c. interpersonal equality
   d. social equality

4. The idea that the law should be applied impartially, without regard for who a person is or who they know is called _____.
   a. legal equity
   b. equality under the law
   c. blind justice
   d. all of the above

5. A _____ society is one in which the power is widely distributed among diverse groups and interests.
   a. elitist
   b. pluralist
   c. democratic
   d. non-authoritative

6. Which of the following is NOT one of the core democratic values?
   a. political equality
   b. political freedom
   c. political participation
   d. majority rule

7. Which of the following is NOT one of the basic values of a representative democracy?
    a. freedom of religion
    b. integrity of the individual
    c. liberty
    d. privacy

8. Major critics of American democracy claim
    a. organized groups do not check and balance each other
    b. politicians are more intersected in manipulating public opinion than following it
    c. that it is elitist
    d. all of the above

9. People voting to decide whether to add an amendment to their constitution is an example of :
    a. democratic substance
    b. democracy as a process
    c. democracy in the populace
    d. popular sovereignty

10. A constitution does all of the following EXCEPT:
    a. establishes the legal relationship between the people and their leaders
    b. determines the rules for attaining power
    c. determines the role of government in the nation's economy
    d. outlines the rules for exercising political power.

11. The Constitutional proposal which called for a bi-cameral legislature was called the:
    a. Virginia plan
    b. Connecticut compromise
    c. New Jersey plan
    d. New York plan

12. The idea that each branch of the government should be responsible for a separate part of the political process is known as:
    a. checks and balances
    b. separation of powers
    c. mixed government
    d. separate responsibilities

13. The U.S. Constitution has been changed in which of the following ways:
    a. custom and usage
    b. formal amendments
    c. legislative interpretation
    d. executive interpretation
    e. all of the above

14. The _____ powers are those listed in the Constitution.
    a. expressed
    b. enumerated
    c. inherent
    d. detailed

15. The power of the president to withhold information based on national security interests in known as:
    a. executive review
    b. executive rights
    c. executive privilege
    d. executive power

16. The power of the courts to determine the constitutionality of actions of the legislative and executive branches is known as _____.
    a. judicial review
    b. judicial interpretation
    c. constitutional review power
    d. all of the above

17. The problems of the Articles of Confederation included all of the following EXCEPT:
    a. the restriction of the national government to raise an army
    b. the inability of the national government to levy taxes
    c. economic rivalry between the states
    d. the lack of a middle class

18. Which of the following were designed to limit the impact of factions in society?
    a. Majority interests were filtered through elected representatives.
    b. The wishes of the majority are diluted by republicanism.
    c. The majority will is buffered by the joint effect of federalism and the separation of powers.
    d. All of the above

19. Which of the following is true of the formal amendment process?
   a. the president can veto amendments.
   b. Amendments can be passed without ever going through Congress or the state legislatures.
   c. In order to pass, a Constitutional proposal must be ratified in all the states.
   d. All proposals must be ratified within two years of initiation in order to become law.

20. The Constitution reflects the Founder's fundamental concerns of:
   a. freedom and liberty
   b. state's rights and personal freedoms
   c. national unity and protection of private property
   d. all of the above

Workbook Chapter 3 – Civil Liberties and Civil Rights

Concepts

Affirmative Action

Bill of Rights

Civil Liberties

Civil Rights

Discrimination

Expansion of Rights

Freedom of Expression

Human Rights

Protected Speech

Racism

Right of Privacy

Rights of the Accused

Segregation

Separate but Equal

Unprotected Speech

Key Terms

Absolutist Approach—The belief that the Founders wanted the First Amendment to be interpreted literally, so that Congress should make "no laws" about the expression of views.

Access—The ability to get into and use public facilities.

Affirmative Action—A policy designed to help women and minorities who have been disadvantaged by past discrimination achieve equality in hiring and school admission decisions by taking extra steps to remove the effects of past discrimination.

Bad Tendency Rule—An approach to determining whether an action should be protected under the First amendment that considers whether the action would have a tendency to produce a negative consequence.

Balancing Test—The view of freedom of expression that states that the obligation to protect the rights must be balanced with the effect on society.

Civil Liberties—Freedoms and protections against arbitrary governmental actions.

Civil Rights—The obligations placed on government to protect the freedom of the people.

Clear and Present Danger Test—An approach to determining whether an action should be protected under the First amendment that considers whether the action poses imminent danger of causing some substantive evil that government has a right to prevent.

De Facto Discrimination—discrimination that is not set forth in the law but occurs because of practice.

De Jure Discrimination—Discrimination that is set forth in law.

Discrimination—Unequal and/or unfair treatment of a person or class of people.

Exclusionary Rule—The rule derived from the Fourth and Fourteenth Amendments that states that evidence obtained from an unreasonable search or seizure cannot be used in federal trials.

Genocide—The killing of an entire race of people.

Grandfather Clause—A technique used to keep certain groups from voting by providing an exemption from the literacy requirement to only those people whose ancestors were entitled to vote in 1866.

Incorporation Doctrine—The process through which the specific guarantees in the Bill of Rights have been binding on the states through the due process clause of the Fourteenth Amendment.

Inevitable Discovery—An exception to the exclusionary rule that states that evidence obtained from an illegal search may be used in court if the evidence would have eventually been discovered through legal means.

Jim Crow—A term used to describe laws designed to prevent African Americans from voting.

Libel—False or defaming statements about someone in print or the media.

Liberties from Government—The Constitutional protections of the people from state actions.

Liberties in Government—The Constitutional protections that pertain to participation in the political process.

Passive Resistance—Nonviolent protest that entails resisting government laws or practices that are believed to be unjust.

Poll Tax—A technique used to keep certain groups from voting by charging a fee to vote.

Preferred Freedoms Doctrine—The idea that the rights provided in the First Amendment are fundamental and that the courts have a greater obligation to protect these rights than others.

Racial Segregation—The separation of people based on their race.

Racism—The preference for and/or discrimination against a particular race of people.

Reverse Discrimination—The claim by some non-minorities that affirmative action policies discriminate against them based on race.

Separate but Equal—A practice of providing separate public facilities for African Americans and whites in order to circumvent the equal protection requirement of the Fourteenth Amendment. The phrase was coined in the decision in the case of *Plessy v. Ferguson* (1896).

Separation of Church and State—The idea that neither the national nor state governments may pass laws that support one religion or all religions or that give preference to one religion over others.

Slander—False or defamatory oral statements about someone.

Suffrage—The right to vote.

Application

1. In your own words, explain the difference between a civil right and civil liberty.

2. Go on line and check out the websites for each of the following groups:

   Human Rights Campaign
   Amnesty International
   Human Rights Watch
   Electronic Frontier Foundation
   WITNESS

   Identify the policy initiatives and the legal reasoning put forth by these groups. Are they claiming these as civil liberties or civil rights?

3. Suppose you and your family have moved to a new town. The majority of the population in the town are a religion other than yours and the public school has a practice of stopping classes several times a day in order for students to pray in that particular religion. You and your siblings attend the school but do not wish to participate in the religious services.

Should you be required to participate in the activity?

What Supreme Court cases could you use to support your argument?

4. Under what circumstances should government be permitted to limit what a person says?

How should this be monitored?

How do we distinguish between political discourse and criticism of elected leaders and threats to democracy?

What if the things said offend or make others uncomfortable?

5. Do you believe in a Constitutional right to privacy? Explain.

Should government be able to regulate your use of your own body in cases of:

Prostitution?

Body piercing?

Refusal of medical care?

The knowing (or unknowing) transference of communicable diseases?

How would you explain a policy which encompasses the answers you provided above?

6. Explain whether you think government should be able to use information (either to prevent or prosecute a crime) which was obtained:

Without a warrant?

From a defendant who did not understand his/her rights?

From a child whose parents were not present at his/her questioning

By tricking a defendant into thinking the police had evidence of a crime which they did not have?

By denying a defendant food or water for an extended period of time?

By the use of torture?

7. Identify the efforts of the NAACP and others to use the courts to end discrimination. Identify specific court cases as well as the responses by the states.

8. Identify the successes and failures of the women's rights movement of the 1960s through 1990s.

9. How is the struggle of Hispanics for civil rights similar to that of African Americans? Identify the major court cases and events.

Multiple Choice Questions

1. The freedom of citizens to make choices with little or no interference from government are known as:

    a. civil rights
    b. civil liberties
    c. basic freedoms
    d. all of the above

2. Liberties that relate to privacy and protect citizens from the state are known as:
    a. liberties in government
    b. liberties from government
    c. liberties in privacy
    d. liberties in process

3. The idea that the specific guarantees of the Bill of Rights extends to the states is known as:
    a. nationalization of the Constitution
    b. nationalization doctrine
    c. incorporation doctrine
    d. none of the above

4. The conditions set by the Supreme Court which must be met if a religious school is to receive governmental support include:
    a. the support cannot impede or advance religion
    b. the support cannot result in excessive entanglement of church and state
    c. the support must be for a secular purpose
    d. all of the above

5. The idea that the first amendment should be interpreted literally in terms of freedom of expression is known as the:
    a. absolutist approach
    b. preferred-freedoms doctrine
    c. literalist approach
    d. all of the above

6. The idea that restrictions on freedom of expression should be considered on a case-by-case basis to determine if restrictions are necessary to protect society is known as the:
    a. balancing test
    b. case-by-case test
    c. societal protection test
    d. absolutist approach

7. Making false or defaming statements about someone in writing is known as:
   a. slander
   b. obscenity
   c. libel
   d. lying in print

8. The basic requirement(s) for proving a libel case include:
   a. harm
   b. publication
   c. identification
   d. all of the above

9. Which of the following dealt with the right to privacy?
   a. *Griswold v. Connecticut*
   b. *Eisenstadt v. Baird*
   c. *Doe v. Bolton*
   d. All of the above

10. The idea that illegally obtained evidence can be used in court if it would have been discovered eventually through legal means is known as:
   a. the exclusionary rule
   b. inevitable discovery
   c. eventual discovery
   d. inclusionary policy

11. Obligations placed on government to protect freedoms through government action are known as:
   a. civil liberties
   b. civil rights
   c. civil obligations
   d. fundamental freedoms

12. The literacy test exemption given to people whose ancestors were able to vote in 1866 was known as the:
   a. grandfather clause
   b. ancestor requirement
   c. ancestor literacy exemption
   d. none of the above

13. The court case in which the Supreme Court declared the policy of "separate but equal" to be unconstitutional was:
    a. *Brown v. Board of Education*
    b. *Missouri ex rel Gaines v. Canada*
    c. *Guinn v. United States*
    d. *University of California v. Bakke*

14. The federal law which prohibited racial segregation in public accommodations was the:
    a. 1965 Voting Rights Act
    b. 1964 Civil Rights Act
    c. 1972 Civil Liberties Act
    d. none of the above

15. Policies the seek to make up for past discrimination and help minorities by providing them with preferential treatment in hiring and educational admission are known as:
    a. preferential policies
    b. anti-discrimination policies
    c. affirmative action policies
    d. all of the above

16. Discrimination set forth in the law is known as:
    a. de jure discrimination
    b. de facto discrimination
    c. legal discrimination
    d. none of the above

17. The court case ruling which prohibited the use of race and ender in public college admissions was:
    a. *Adarand Constructors Inc. v. Pena*
    b. *University of California v. Bakke*
    c. *Hopwood v. Texas*
    d. None of the above

18. The Supreme Court case which extended the Fourteenth Amendment to homosexuals was:
    a. *Romer v. Evans*
    b. *Bowers v. Hardwick*
    c. *White v. Register*
    d. None of the above

19. The amendment which gave women the right to vote is the:
    a. twelfth
    b. seventeenth
    c. eighteenth
    d. nineteenth

20. The amendment which prohibits states from passing laws which would deny any person "equal protection of the laws" is the:
    a. fourteenth
    b. seventeenth
    c. eighteenth
    d. nineteenth

Workbook Chapter 4 - Congress

Concepts

Bicameralism

Committees

Distribution of Power in the House

Distribution of Power in the Senate

Functions of Congress

Incumbency

Lawmaking

Leadership

Party Government

Pay and Perquisites

Representation

Socio-economic Characteristics of Members of Congress

Key Terms

Administrative Assistant—The Congressional office employee responsible for the overall management of the office.

Allocation Responsiveness—Representation in which members of Congress ensure their district gets a share of federal benefits.

Appointment Secretary—The Congressional office employee responsible for maintaining the appointment calendar of the member of Congress.

Bicameral—A legislature with two chambers.

Casework—The tasks legislators perform based on the requests and needs of their constituents.

Caseworkers—The Congressional office employee responsible for helping constituents with problems they are having with government.

Caucus—A conference of all the party members in a chamber that is responsible for assigning party members to committees.

Censure—The verbal reprimand of a member of Congress by the House or Senate, which involves the member standing in front of the chamber while the censure, is read aloud.

Closed rule—The rule that prohibits amending a bill when it is on the floor of the House or Senate for consideration.

Cloture—A procedure of the Senate to end a filibuster by a vote of sixty senators.

Committee of the Whole—The name given to the House of Representatives when it considers a bill under less formal rules.

Conditional Party Government—The granting of power to majority party leaders by rank and file party members who form a cohesive majority and the expectation that party leaders will use the power to enact the party's legislative agenda.

Conferees—Members of a conference committee.

Conference Committee—A temporary congressional committee made up of members of the House and Senate that meets to reconcile the differences in legislation as it passes each chamber.

Delegate—A representative who makes legislative decisions based on the interests and views of his/her constituents, regardless of personal preference.

Discharge Petition—A procedure of the House of Representatives that permits the members to bring a bill out of committee and directly to the floor if they get 218 signatures on a petition.

Exclude—The refusal of Congress to seat any candidate who wins election but does not meet the constitutional requirements to hold congressional office.

Exclusive Committees—Committees whose members are not given any other committee assignments.

Expulsion—The removal of a member of Congress from office.

Filibuster—The effort by a Senator to delay the chamber's business by making long speeches.

Floor Leader—A term used to describe the majority and minority leaders.

Franking Privilege—The ability of members of Congress to send mail to their constituents free of charge.

Hold—The formal request by a member of the Senate to be notified prior to any bill coming to the floor.

Home Style—The way a member of Congress behaves, explains their legislative actions, and presents themselves in their district.

Johnson Rule—The rule that no member of the Senate may receive a second seat on a major committee until each member has been given one.

Joint Committee—A congressional committee made up of members of the House and Senate.

Legislative Assistant—The congressional office employee responsible for keeping the member of Congress informed about specific policy issues.

Legislative Correspondent—The congressional office employee responsible for answering the mail from constituents.

Legislative Director—The congressional office employee who supervises the legislative assistants.

Major Committee—Committees in Congress that are responsible for specific policy areas but which are not as prestigious as the top committees.

Majority Leader—The person, chosen by the members of the majority party, who controls the legislative agenda; the majority leader is the most powerful person in the chamber.

Majority Whip—The representative of the majority party in the House who helps keep the party members informed of the party's position on issues and encourages them to vote the way the party would like.

Minority Leader—The person chosen by the members of the minority party to coordinate communication among party members in the House or Senate.

Minority Whip—The representative of the minority party in the House or Senate who helps keep the party members informed of the party's position on issues and encourages them to vote the way the party would like.

Modified Rules—Rules that permit consideration of some but not all amendments to a bill when it is on the floor of the chamber.

Multiple Referral—A practice in the House and Senate permitting a bill to be referred to more than one committee.

Nongermane Amendments—An amendment that is not related to the subject of the bill to which it is added.

Norm Of Reciprocity—The custom of congressional committee members to respect the work and judgments of other committees.

Open Rule—The rule that permits any germane amendment to be added to a piece of legislation.

Party Committees—Committees that coordinate party activities in Congress.

Party Ratio—The proportion of the chamber each political party controls.

Perquisites (Perks)—The benefits and support that members of Congress receive to help them perform their job.

Policy Responsiveness—This refers to the amount of agreement between the people represented and their elected officials on policy issues.

Pork-barrel Benefits—Federal government benefits given to congressional districts based on the efforts of members of Congress.

President of the Senate—The Vice President of the United States, who presides over the Senate and is responsible for such parliamentary duties as recognizing speakers and voting to break ties.

President Pro Tempore—The person chosen by the members to preside over the Senate in the absence of the Vice President.

Press Secretary—The congressional office employee responsible for handling press relations.

Representation—The relationship between elected officials and the people who put them in office.

Reprimand—An action in the House of Representatives in which a statement criticizing a member is read before the chamber.

Rider—Amendments (possibly nongermane) added to a popular bill in hopes that the desirability of the proposed legislation will help the amendment be passed.

Select Committee—A temporary congressional committee formed to deal with a specific issue.

Service Responsiveness—Representation that takes the form of the tasks legislators perform based on the requests and needs of their constituents.

Speaker of the House of Representatives—The person who presides over the House, is responsible for the many of the parliamentary duties such as recognizing speakers, and is the most powerful person in the chamber.

Standing Committees—Permanent congressional committees that are responsible for legislation in a specific policy area.

Subcommittee—A subdivision of a committee designed to provide an additional division of labor and specializing.

Symbolic Responsiveness—The use of political symbols to generate trust and support among the voters.

Top Committees—The committees in the House and Senate that are desired by most legislators.

Trustee—Representatives who use their own judgment in legislative decisions.

Unanimous Consent Agreements—An agreement on the procedures and conditions under which a bill will be considered in the Senate negotiated by party leaders and agreed upon by Senators.

Unicameral—A legislature with one chamber.

Unrequested Committees—Committees few members of Congress want to serve on.

Whips—Assistants to the majority and minority leaders who help keep party members informed of the party's position on issues and encourage them to vote the way the party would like.

Application

1. Go on line to the US House of Representatives website. Find the link to the committees. Select a committee you find interesting. In your own words explain the jurisdiction or responsibility of that committee. List the names, party, and states of the committee members.

Committee: _____

Member Name	Party	State & District

How might these different constituencies lead to conflict over legislation in the House of Representatives? Are there any sources of cooperation in the district constituencies?

2. Go on-line to the Project Vote Smart website. Look up the descriptions of the Congressional districts for a representative from South Dakota and one from Los Angeles.

South Dakota Representative Name _____

    District # _____ Date first elected _____

    Previous Political Experience_____

Los Angeles Representative Name _____

    District # _____ Date first elected _____

    Previous Political Experience_____

3. In your own words, explain the different types of responsiveness (symbolic, allocation & service).

4. Now go to the website for your member of Congress. What actions/efforts does he/she list that could be described at symbolic, allocation and service responsiveness?

U.S. Representative Name	District Number	Actions
	Symbolic	
	Allocation	
	Service	

5. Fill in the blanks:

	Name	Party	State/District	Job description
President Pro Tempore				
Majority Leader of the Senate				
Minority Whip of the Senate				
Speaker of the House				
Minority Leader in the House				
Majority Whip in the House				

6. Imagine you are the legislative director of an interest group and a bill has been proposed in Congress which would be disastrous for your group. Using your book and your own knowledge of the legislative process, list where in Congress you might try to stop the legislation and how you might do that.

7. Imagine yourself the newly elected Senator from the state of Texas. What committee assignment would you request?

Explain why you have selected this committee.

If you have chosen a prestigious committee, explain how/why you might get this assignment.

8. What are the advantages and disadvantages of members of Congress serving for many years in the House or Senate? Would you recommend your state place term limits on its delegation in the House or Senate?

9. List and briefly explain 6 things Congress can do to limit the influence of the President, the bureaucracy, and the Supreme Court.

      1.

      2.

      3.

      4.

      5.

      6.

10. Explain how the terms of office in the House and Senate can influence how these chambers interact.

11. Describe the professional qualifications and profile the typical member of Congress.

12. Explain how the size of the House and Senate can influence how business is conducted on the floor of each chamber.

13. Identify and describe the role of committees in the House and Senate. What are the advantages and disadvantages of using committees?

1. The primary functions of Congress include all of the following EXCEPT:
   a. overseeing government programs
   b. informing the public
   c. impeachment
   d. legislating

2. The secondary functions of Congress include:
   a. disciplining members
   b. confirmation of the vice president when there is a vacancy in office
   c. impeachment
   d. all of the above

3. Representation is comprised of :
   a. service responsiveness
   b. policy responsiveness
   c. symbolic responsiveness
   d. all of the above

4. When members of Congress provide services to their constituents it is known as:
   a. symbolic responsiveness
   b. service responsiveness
   c. constituent responsiveness
   d. policy responsiveness

5. Representatives who use their own judgments when making voting decision are known as:
   a. delegates
   b. trustees
   c. politicos
   d. none of the above

6. When Congress refuses to seat a person who has won election to Congress it is known as:
   a. expulsion
   b. censure
   c. exclusion
   d. reprimand

7. When Congress passes a resolution reprimanding a member's behavior it is known as:
    a. expulsion
    b. censure
    c. exclusion
    d. reprimand

8. Congressional staff typically include:
    a. legislative correspondent
    b. appointment secretary
    c. legislative director
    d. administrative assistant
    e. all of the above

9. The Congressional staff person who is responsible for answering constituent mail is known as:
    a. legislative correspondent
    b. appointment secretary
    c. legislative director
    d. administrative assistant

10. The Senator who is chosen by his/her colleagues to preside over the Senate when the Vice President is absent is known as:
    a. majority leader
    b. president of the Senate
    c. president pro tempore
    d. whip

11. Committees have a powerful influence over legislation because:
    a. committee members are more interested in legislation than non-committee members
    b. committee members are more knowledgeable about legislation than non-committee members
    c. there is a norm of reciprocity in Congress
    d. all of the above

12. Committees to which few members seek assignment, such as House Administration and Government Reform, are known as:
    a. unrequested committees
    b. top committees
    c. major committees
    d. prestigious committees

13. The longstanding practice in the Senate that no member will serve on more than two major committees at a time is known as the:
    a. major committee rule
    b. committee rule
    c. Johnson rule
    d. Jones rule

14. When a bill is sent to the floor of the House and germane amendments are permitted on the floor, it is said to be under the:
    a. open rule
    b. closed rule
    c. germane rule
    d. modified rule

15. Committees made of members of the House and Senate whose purpose is to reconcile the differences in versions of a bill passed in each chamber are known as:
    a. party committees
    b. joint committees
    c. conference committees
    d. caucus

16. When a Senator requests that he/she be notified when a bill comes to the floor and in essence tells the Senate that there are objections to the bill, it is known as a:
    a. filibuster
    b. notification
    c. warning
    d. hold

17. When two or more committees have jurisdiction over a legislative proposal it is known as:
    a. multiple referral
    b. overlapping jurisdiction
    c. jurisdiction sharing
    d. none of the above

18. When a bill is removed from a committee against the wishes of the committee members, it is known as:
    a. a removal petition
    b. cloture
    c. a discharge petition
    d. all of the above

19. In overseeing government administration, Congress may:
    a. withhold funding for government programs
    b. create new executive branch agencies
    c. assign a program to an agency
    d. all of the above

20. A legislature with two chambers is known as:
    a. unicameral
    b. bicameral
    c. a Congress
    d. none of the above

Workbook Chapter 5 - Presidency

Concepts

Cabinet

Expansion of Presidential Power

Formal Powers

Informal Powers

Presidency as an Organization

President as Opinion Leader

President as Party Leader

Presidential Approval Ratings

Presidential Management Styles

Presidential Personality

Presidential Success in Congress

Views of Presidential Power

Key Terms

Active-Negative—A way of classifying presidents based on personality as someone who is concerned with attaining political power for its own sake.

Active-Positive—A way of classifying presidents based on personality as someone who derives great satisfaction from holding office and will be active in their efforts to govern.

Active Presidents—A way of classifying presidents based on personality as someone who invests a great deal of energy into the office and whose skills and personal needs make them well suited for political leadership.

Council of Economic Advisors—An agency of the Executive Office of the President that is responsible for advising the president on the U.S. economy.

Executive Agreements—An agreement between the United States and other nations, created by the president and have the same weight as a treaty, but do not require senatorial approval.

Going Public—A strategy of the president that calls for him to appeal to the public in an effort to accomplish his political goals.

Hierarchical Model—A method of organizing the presidency that calls for clear lines of authority and delegates responsibility from the president and through the chief of staff.

Major Address—A presidential speech on a substantive policy or political issue delivered directly to the nation.

Minor Address—A presidential speech on a substantive policy or political issue delivered to a specific audience.

National Security Council—A group of presidential advisors made up of the vice president, attorney general, and cabinet officers chosen by the president to advise him on national security issues and which is part of the Executive Office of the President.

Negative President—A way of classifying presidents based on personality as someone who serves as president out of a sense of obligation rather than pleasure.

Office of Management and Budget—An agency of the Executive Office of the President that is responsible for assisting the president in creating the budget.

Passive-Negative—A way of classifying presidents based on personality as someone who has a deep sense of civic responsibility and is not particularly aggressive in governing.

Passive-Positive—A way of classifying presidents based on personality as someone who is primarily interested in popularity and less interested in governing.

Passive Presidents—A way of classifying presidents based on personality as someone who invests little time or energy into the office and who is not well suited for political leadership.

Pocket Veto—The veto resulting from a president taking no action on legislation that has passed Congress after Congress has adjourned

Positive Government—The idea that government should play a major role in preventing or dealing with the crises that face the nation.

Positive Presidents—A way of classifying presidents based on personality as someone who derives great satisfaction from holding office.

Prerogative View—A view of presidential power promoted by Abraham Lincoln, which argues that the president is required to preserve the Constitution and take actions to do so which might otherwise be unconstitutional.

Restrictive View—A view of presidential power that argues that the president may exercise only those powers listed in the Constitution.

Spokes-of-the-Wheel Model—A method of organizing the presidency that calls for the president to be the center of activity with numerous advisors reporting directly to the president.

Stewardship Doctrine—A view of presidential power that states that the president is a steward of the people and should do anything the nation needs which are not prohibited by the Constitution.

Strong-Executive Model—A model of the presidency in which the powers of the executive office are significant and independent from Congress.

Weak-Executive Model—A model of the presidency in which the job of the executive is primarily to carry out the decisions of Congress.

White House Office—A section of the Executive Office of the Presidency which contains the offices of many of the most influential advisors to the president.

Application

1. Go on line to the Gallop Poll (www.gallup.com). What is the president's most recent approval rating?

   What was the question used to ascertain the president's approval rating?

   Is the president's approval rating increasing or decreasing?

   Why would the approval rating matter to the president, his opponents and those supporting his legislative agenda?

   How/why is popularity a resource?

2. Go on line and find an Electoral College map of the United States (make sure it is up to date!). Write down the site you used and answer the following:

_____

State	Number of Electors?
Texas	
Arkansas	
North Dakota	
California	
Ohio	

Given the allocation of electors seen above, explain the electoral strategy you would recommend to a presidential candidate? In which states should presidential candidates spend their time or not?

Spend Time	Do Not Spend Time

Now look at how the states voted in the last presidential election. How does that modify your strategy if the candidate you are advising is a Republican? If he/she is a Democrat?

Republican	Democrat

74

3. How does the president as a party leader affect the performance of the president in other areas of responsibility?

4. List the formal and informal powers of the president. Go to the White House website (www.whitehouse.gov) and find 5 policy ideas that the president supports.
    - Identify which formal power he could use to accomplish this goal.
    - Identify which informal power he could use to accomplish this goal.

POLICY INIATIVE	FORMAL POWER	INFORMAL POWER

5. Identify, describe, and diagram the different methods of organizing the presidency.

6. Describe how the president's relationship with the media and his *publics* change throughout his tenure in office.

7. Go to the White House website (www.whitehouse.gov) and explore the presidency as an organization. Answer the following:

OFFICE	OFFICE HOLDER (Name)	WHAT DOES THIS PERSON DO?	HOW DOES THIS PERSON HELP THE PRESIDENT?
White House Chief of Staff			
White House Press Secretary			
National Security Advisor			
Secretary of State			
Secretary of Treasury			

Multiple Choice Questions

1. The model of the executive which calls for the president to simply implement the decisions of Congress and have a strictly limited terms is known as:
    a. strong-executive model.
    b. weak-executive model.
    c. U.S. Presidential model.
    d. modified-executive model.

2. Which of the following is responsible for the expansion of presidential power?
    a. vague constitution provisions which have been interpreted to give presidents more power
    b. congressional delegation of power
    c. changing expectations of the presidency
    d. all of the above

3. The view of the presidency which calls for the president to exercise only those powers specifically listed in the Constitution is known as:
    a. prerogative view.
    b. stewardship view.
    c. restrictive view.
    d. limited view.

4. The personality type that describes presidents as being preoccupied with seeking power for its own sake is known as:
    a. passive-positive.
    b. passive-negative.
    c. active-positive.
    d. active-negative.

5. Which of the following is NOT a component of the presidency as an organization?
    a. the first lady
    b. the cabinet
    c. the press
    d. the Executive Office of the President

6. Which of the following is part of the Executive Office of the President?
    a. the National Security Council
    b. the Office of Management and Budget
    c. the Council of Economic Advisors
    d. all of the above

7. The model of organizing the White House Staff which calls for the president to be at the center of the organization with advisors reporting directly to him is known as:
    a. spokes-of-the-wheel model.
    b. hierarchical model.
    c. direct power model.
    d. none of the above.

8. Which of the following is NOT one of the primary constitutional responsibilities of the president:
    a. chief executive.
    b. chief diplomat.
    c. party leader.
    d. commander in chief.

9. When the Constitution grants that the president shall make sure that the laws are "faithfully executed" it makes the president the:
    a. chief executive.
    b. chief diplomat.
    c. party leader.
    d. commander in chief.

10. When a president enters into an agreement with another nation without the creation of a treaty or congressional approval it is known as:
    a. an illegal use of diplomatic power.
    b. an executive agreement.
    c. an unconstitutional expansion of presidential power.
    d. all of the above.

11. Which of the following is a limitation on the president's ability to act as his party's leader?
    a. the separation of branches in the national government
    b. the rise of direct primaries
    c. the mistrust of parties by the public
    d. all of the above

12. When presidents appeal to the public in an effort to circumvent other political actors it is known as:
    a. going to the people.
    b. going around the power.
    c. going public.
    d. all of the above.

13. Presidents can make direct appeals to the public through the use of:
    a. personal trips.
    b. minor addresses.
    c. the press.
    d. all of the above.

14. All of the following are important determinants of presidential approval ratings EXCEPT:
    a. scandal.
    b. the economy.
    c. congressional success.
    d. international crisis.

15. The pocket veto:
    a. can only happen when Congress is not in session.
    b. requires the president to neither sign or veto a bill.
    c. has the effect of a veto.
    d. all of the above.

16. All of the following influence presidential – congressional relations EXCEPT:
    a. electoral constituencies.
    b. party and ideology.
    c. presidential popularity.
    d. all of the above.

17. The informal methods of the president influencing legislation include:
    a. systematic lobbying.
    b. patronage.
    c. the power to persuade.
    d. all of the above.

18. The idea that government should play a major role in meeting and preventing most major problems faced by society is known as:
    a. positive government.
    b. activist government.
    c. pro-active government.
    d. presidential government.

19. The power of the president to appoint the heads of the executive branch agencies falls under which power?
    a. chief diplomat
    b. chief executive
    c. chief administrator
    d. chief legislator

20. A presidential speech on a topic of national importance and delivered to a national audience is known as:
  a. national address.
  b. State of the Union address.
  c. major address.
  d. minor address.

Workbook Chapter 6 – The Federal Courts

Concepts

Access

Appeal

Fact Finding

Independent Courts

Judicial Organization

Judicial Power

Judicial Review

Judicial Selection and Confirmation

Jurisdiction

Legal Reasoning

Models of Judicial Decision Making

Opinion

Political Jurisprudence

Precedent

Key Terms

Collegial Courts—Court in which a group of judges decide cases based on a review of the records of lower court trials.

Concurrent Jurisdiction—Jurisdiction in which both state and federal courts are entitled to hear a particular type of case.

Concurring Opinion—Opinion written by Supreme Court justices who agree with the ruling of the Court but not the reason behind it.

Conference—The meeting in which Supreme Court justices decide which cases they will hear.

Constitutional Interpretation—An action in which the Supreme Court determines whether a law is in compliance with the Constitution.

Courts of Appellate Jurisdiction—Courts that review the decisions of lower courts.

Courts of Original Jurisdiction—Trial courts that hear cases for the first time and determine issues of fact and law.

Dissenting Opinion—Opinion written by Supreme Court justices who opposed the majority opinion.

En Banc—An action of a collegial court in which a case is heard by the entire court.

Exclusive Jurisdiction—When a court is the only court that can hear a case.

Judicial Activism—Supreme Court decision making in which the Court takes an active role in policy making through interpretation of the Constitution.

Judicial Conference—A committee of district and appellate judges that reviews the needs of the federal judiciary and makes recommendations to Congress.

Judicial Power—The power of the courts to interpret and apply the law.

Judicial Restraint—Supreme Court decision making in which the Court leaves policymaking to the other branches of government.

Judicial Review—The power of a court to review decision of the lower courts and to determine the constitutionality of laws and actions of public officials.

Jurisdiction—The types of cases a given court is permitted to hear.

Legal Realist—Judicial decision making in which judges balance existing laws and precedents with the effect their decisions will have on society.

Legislative Interpretation—Supreme Court ruling on the meaning and intent of an action of Congress.

Majority Opinion—Supreme Court decision in which five or more justices agree on a ruling and on the reason for the ruling.

Original Intent—The idea that Supreme Court justices should interpret the Constitution in terms of the original intentions of the framers.

Plurality Opinion—Supreme Court decision in which a majority of the justices agree on a decision but not the reason for the decision.

Rule of Four—Four Supreme Court justices are required to agree to hear a case.

Senatorial Courtesy—The practice of having senators from the president's political party recommend District Court nominees.

Slot Machine Theory—The view of judicial review in which the court determines whether a law is constitutional by comparing the relevant constitutional provision with the law being challenged to determine if the two coincide.

Standing to Sue—The legal right to bring a lawsuit based on having a stake in the outcome.

Writ of Certiorari—An action stating that the Supreme Court will hear a case that has been appealed to them.

Writ of Mandamus—A court order instructing an elected official to carry out an official duty.

Application

1. For each of the following hypothetical cases, determine whether the case would be heard on the state or federal level?

Case	State Jurisdiction	Federal Jurisdiction
A speeding ticket on an interstate highway		
A case in which a citizen sues the Environmental Protection Agency		
A Texas citizen has an issue with the North American Free Trade Agreement		
A dispute between Louisiana and Mississippi over off-shore oil drilling		
A state law which prohibits parents from taking their children to certain non-Christian churches		

2. Explain the method of judicial selection on the federal level. What are the advantages and disadvantages of this method?

3. In your own words, explain the various models of judicial decision making.

Legal Realist Model

Attitudinal Model

Strategic Model

4. Explain the logic for and ways to balance the courts.

5. Explain in your own words, the constraints on judicial review.

6. List the ways in which judges and courts make public policy.

7. In your own words explain the difference between original and appellate jurisdiction.

8. Describe the role of precedent in judicial decision making.

9. Identify the internal and external checks on judicial power.

10. Describe the procedures for fact finding in the court system.

Multiple Choice Questions

1. The authority of the courts to interpret and apply the law is known as:
   a. judicial review.
   b. judicial power.
   c. lawmaking power.
   d. none of the above.

2. Congress may set the jurisdictional boundaries of the federal courts by:
   a. allowing federal and state courts concurrent jurisdiction.
   b. assigning exclusive jurisdiction.
   c. forbidding the courts to handle a certain type of case.
   d. all of the above.

3. The right of state and federal courts to both hear a particular case is known as:
   a. concurrent jurisdiction.
   b. shared jurisdiction.
   c. national jurisdiction.
   d. none of the above.

4. The power to review the actions of lower courts and declare laws and actions of public officials unconstitutional is known as:
   a. judicial supremacy.
   b. constitutional interpretation power.
   c. constitutional review.
   d. judicial review.

5. The committee of district and appellate judges which reviews the needs of the federal judiciary and makes recommendations to Congress is known as:
   a. judicial needs committee.
   b. judicial-congressional relations committee.
   c. judicial conference.
   d. none of the above.

6. Courts in which a group of judges review the record of the lower court trial are known as:
   a. review courts.
   b. collegial courts.
   c. district courts.
   d. all of the above.

7. When the Supreme Court issues an opinion in which five or more justices agree on which side wins and the reason for that decision it is known as a:
    a. clear opinion.
    b. plurality opinion.
    c. concurring opinion.
    d. majority opinion.

8. When an opinion is written by the justices in the minority on a particular case it is known as:
    a. concurring opinion.
    b. minority opinion.
    c. dissenting opinion.
    d. plurality opinion.

9. Common expectations of federal judges include all of the following EXCEPT:
    a. they are neither too young or too old.
    b. they have had a career in public service.
    c. they are wealthy.
    d. they have legal training.

10. The practice of potential judges being recommended by senators or house members of the president's political party is known as:
    a. congressional courtesy.
    b. senatorial courtesy.
    c. senatorial privilege.
    d. congressional privilege.

11. When appointing justices to the Supreme Court, efforts to balance the court have focused on:
    a. race and ethnicity.
    b. geography.
    c. religion.
    d. all of the above.

12. A court order instructing a public official to perform an official duty is known as a:
    a. *writ of certiorari.*
    b. *writ of mandamus.*
    c. *writ of habeas corpus.*
    d. *writ of replevin.*

13. The idea that judicial review should be limited to determining if the statute in question squares with the constitutional provision is known as:
    a. legal realist theory.
    b. slot machine theory.
    c. squares theory.
    d. none of the above.

14. When the Supreme Court defers policymaking authority to the other branches of government it is known as:
    a. judicial deferment.
    b. judicial activism.
    c. judicial restraint.
    d. none of the above.

15. The constraints on judicial review include all of the following EXCEPT:
    a. impeachment.
    b. self-restraint.
    c. constitutional amendments.
    d. removal of congressional funding.

16. For a case to heard in federal court the subject matter must concern:
    a. the Constitution.
    b. a treaty.
    c. maritime matters.
    d. any of the above.

17. The federal court(s) which are trial courts with original jurisdiction are:
    a. the Supreme Court.
    b. the district courts.
    c. the Court of Appeals.
    d. all of the above.

18. The idea that judges' personal values are good indicators of how he/she will rule on cases is known as the:
    a. attitudinal model.
    b. legal model.
    c. values model.
    d. none of the above.

19. Judicial review:
  a. was most clearly set forth in *Marbury v. Madison.*
  b. was debated by the framers in the Federalist papers.
  c. when applied to the actions of elected officials, can be considered undemocratic.
  d. all of the above.

20. When federal judges are removed from office by Congress it is known as:
  a. congressional removal.
  b. impeachment.
  c. judicial constraint.
  d. none of the above.

Workbook Chapter 7 - Bureaucracy

Concepts

Bureaucracy as a Model of Organization

Bureaucratic Power

Functions of the Bureaucracy

Growth of Bureaucracy

Neutral Competence

Oversight

Reforming Bureaucracy

Staffing the Bureaucracy

Structure of the Bureaucracy

Types of Bureaucratic Agencies

Key Terms

Adjudication—The process of determining if a law has been broken.

Advisory Committees—A temporary or permanent organization created to provide information and technical expertise to the bureaucracy.

Agency Capture—A term used to describe when an agency seems to operate to the benefit of those who it is supposed to regulate.

Appointment—A power of the president that enables him to control the bureaucracy by selecting the people who will head its agencies.

Bureaucracy—The term used to refer to the agencies of the federal government. It also refers to an organizational framework and has negative connotations.

Cabinet Departments—The fifteen largest and most influential agencies of the federal bureaucracy.

Clientele Departments—A type of bureaucratic agency created primarily as a result of the pressure of interest groups that tends to serve their interests.

Council of Economic Advisors—An agency of the Executive Office of the President that is responsible for advising the President on the U.S. economy.

Due Process—The procedural safeguards used to ensure that people are treated fairly in the adjudication process.

Essential Functions—The most basic and necessary functions of government for which the departments of the treasury, state and defense were created.

Executive Office of the President—The agency that is responsible for managing all the other agencies of the executive branch for the President.

Executive Orders—Directives of the president that have the same weight as law and were not voted on by Congress.

Fire Alarm Oversight—Oversight that becomes active only when there is evidence of bureaucratic wrongdoing.

Fourth Branch of Government—A term used to describe the federal bureaucracy.

Government Corporations—Federally established businesses that are narrow in focus and are in part self-supporting.

Impoundment—The limited ability of the president to not spend money appropriated by Congress.

Independent Agencies—Agencies of the federal bureaucracy that are smaller and have a more narrow focus and purpose than the cabinet agencies.

Iron Triangle—A term used to refer to the inter-dependent relationship between the bureaucracy, interest groups and congressional committees.

Legislative Intent—The intention of Congress when it passes laws.

Legislative Vetoes—The ability of Congress to reject an action or decision of the bureaucracy.

Merit System—A system of governing in which jobs are given based on relevant technical expertise and the ability to perform.

National Needs—The creation of agencies to provide for the needs of the nation.

National Security Council—A group of presidential advisors made up of the Vice President, Attorney General, and cabinet officers chosen by the president to advise him on national security issues and which is part of the Executive Office of the President.

Neutral Competence—The idea that agencies should make decisions based on expertise rather than political considerations.

Office of Management and Budget—An agency of the Executive Office of the President that is responsible for assisting the president in creating the budget.

Overhead Democracy—The idea that the bureaucracy is controlled through the oversight of elected officials, who are chosen by the people, thus giving the populace control over the bureaucracy.

Police Patrol Oversight—The active oversight of the bureaucracy by elected officials to make sure that they are acting according to the wishes of the people.

Principal-Agent Model—A model explaining the relationship between Congress and the bureaucracy, which states the relationship is similar to that between an employer who seeks to have work done and an employee who does the work.

Rule—A statement of the bureaucracy that interprets the law or prescribes a specific action.

Rulemaking—The process of the bureaucracy deciding what the laws passed by Congress mean and how they should be carried out.

Standards of Due Process—The procedural guarantees provided to ensure fair treatment and Constitutional rights.

Spoils System—A system of governing in which political positions and benefits are given to the friends of the winner.

Sunshine Laws—Laws intended to keep the bureaucracy accountable to the people by requiring that agency meetings be open to the public.

White House Office—A section of the Executive Office of the Presidency which houses many of the most influential advisors to the president.

Application

1. Imagine you were given the task of creating a new federal agency intended to regulate the banking industry. What type of agency structure (cabinet department, government corporation, etc.) would you recommend? Why?

2. Imagine you were given the task of dealing with the recent cases of regulatory failure in the food industry (tainted peanut butter, e-coli in the lettuce crop). Using your knowledge of iron triangles explain how you might improve regulation.

3. In your own words explain the tools the President and Congress can use to control the bureaucracy.

4. Go on-line and look up each of the following agencies. List the purpose of the agency as well as the name of the agency head.

AGENCY	PURPOSE	AGENCY HEAD
Federal Emergency Management Agency		
Secret Service		
Alcohol Tobacco & Firearms		
National Security Agency		
Department of Energy		

5. Explain in your own words why the U.S. Federal bureaucracy has become so powerful.

6. In your own words, explain bureaucracy as a model of organization. What are its characteristics and what are the advantages to this form of organization?

7. In your own words describe the role of the bureaucracy in rulemaking and policy formation.

8. Identify and describe the differences between cabinet agencies, independent agencies, and regulatory commissions.

Multiple Choice Questions

1. All of the following are components of the Weberian model of bureaucracy EXCEPT:
    a. Professionalization.
    b. spoils system.
    c. division of labor.
    d. formal rules.

2. The assignment of government jobs based on "who you know" rather than relevant technical qualifications is known as:
    a. the spoils system.
    b. the merit system.
    c. connections.
    d. none of the above.

3. The idea that public agencies should make decisions based on expertise rather than personal or political considerations is known as:
    a. professionalism.
    b. unbiased rulemaking.
    c. neutral competence.
    d. all of the above.

4. The agencies which are charged with the responsibility of carrying out federal programs in general policy areas and tend to be the best known to the public are the:
    a. independent agencies.
    b. government corporations.
    c. Executive Office of the President.
    d. cabinet departments.

5. Agencies which are neither purely private nor public institutions are known as:
    a. cabinet departments.
    b. government corporations.
    c. quasi-public agencies.
    d. independent agencies.

6. The process of deciding what the laws passed by Congress mean is known as:
    a. adjudication.
    b. clarification.
    c. rulemaking.
    d. discretionary interpretation.

7. When an agency acts somewhat like a court and decides if a law has been broken it is known as:
    a. adjudication.
    b. clarification.
    c. rulemaking.
    d. discretionary interpretation.

8. Bureaucracies influence policy formation through:
    a. lobbying.
    b. use of expertise.
    c. alliances with important clientele.
    d. all of the above.

9. Which of the following was NOT part of the evolution of cabinet departments?
    a. they were created in response to national needs
    b. they provided the essential functions of government
    c. they were created in response to the needs of clientele groups
    d. they were created to provide support services for the legislative branch

10. The idea that elected officials hold the bureaucracy accountable out of fear of electoral response on the part of the public is known as:
    a. overhead democracy.
    b. electoral accountability.
    c. bureaucratic electoral control.
    d. oversight.

11. When Congressional oversight becomes active after some evidence of bureaucratic wrongdoing it is known as:
    a. police patrol oversight.
    b. response based oversight.
    c. fire alarm oversight.
    d. retroactive oversight.

12. When an agency appears to run simply for the benefit of those it is supposed to regulate it is known as:
    a. iron triangle.
    b. regulatory bias.
    c. agency-industry regulation.
    d. agency capture.

13. The requirement that bureaucratic decisions be made at open meetings is known as:
    a. open meeting requirements.
    b. sunset requirements.
    c. freedom of information requirements.
    d. sunshine laws.

14. Congress can control the bureaucracy through use of:
    a. legislation.
    b. appropriations.
    c. legislative veto.
    d. all of the above.

15. The President can control the bureaucracy using all of the following EXCEPT:
    a. impoundment.
    b. veto.
    c. appointment.
    d. executive orders.

16. Bureaucracies are difficult to reform because:
    a. they control the information and expertise.
    b. agencies are popular, even if bureaucracy is not.
    c. government is not a business.
    d. all of the above.

17. When a court has to determine if an agency's actions are permitted by the laws passed by Congress, the court is judging:
    a. standards of due process.
    b. legislative intent.
    c. legislative authority.
    d. none of the above.

18. When the President attempts to control the bureaucracy by refusing to spend money appropriated by Congress it is known as:
    a. financial control.
    b. executive order control.
    c. impoundment.
    d. all of the above.

19. Which of the commonly held beliefs about the federal bureaucracy is true?
    a. they are inefficient
    b. they are located primarily in Washington D.C.
    c. they do not reflect the general public in terms of race and gender
    d. all of the above are true

20. Which of the following is NOT part of the Executive Office of the Presidency?
   a. National Security Council
   b. Office of Management and Budget
   c. Council of Economic Advisors
   d. Department of Labor

Workbook Chapter 8 – Political Parties

Concepts

Characteristics of the American Party System

Conservative

Functions of Political Parties

Liberal

Minor Party

Organization and Structure of Political Parties

Party Affiliation

Party Amateur

Party Competition

Party Professional

Primary Election

Key Terms

Amateurs—People who participate in the activities of political parties based primarily on purposive or social incentives.

Critical Election—The first election that clearly reflects a new partisan alignment that produces a new partisan majority.

Direct Primary—The selection of a party's candidate by a vote of party members.

Divided Government—When one party controls the Presidency and another controls Congress.

Electoral Realignment—new and sustaining pattern of partisan loyalties.

Initiative—A type of election in which voters are asked to make policy decisions.

Minor Party—Political parties that periodically appear but have little success in winning office.

Multimember Constituencies—A method of selecting representatives in which more than one person is chosen to represent a single constituency.

Multiparty System—A political system in which three or more political parties effectively compete for political office and no one party can win control of all.

One-Party System—A political system in which representatives of one political party hold all or almost all of the major offices in government.

Parliamentary System—An electoral system which the party holding the majority selects the chief executive and has the effect of encouraging multiple parties.

Party Discipline—Requiring political party members in public office to promote or carry out the party's agenda and punishing those who do not.

Party in Government—The component of a political party that is made up of elected and appointed government officeholders who belong to a political party.

Party in the Electorate—The component of a political party that is made up of the people in the public who identify with a political party.

Party Organization—The component of a political party that is comprised of the party professionals who hold official positions in the party.

Party Vote—A vote in which a majority of Democrats vote on one side and a majority of Republicans vote on the other.

Political Machine—A political organization characterized by a reciprocal relationship between voters and officeholders. Political support is given in exchange for government jobs and services.

Political Patronage—The giving of government jobs to people based on their party affiliation and loyalty.

Political Party—An organization that nominates and runs candidates for public office under its own name.

Presidential System—A political system in which the chief executive and the legislature are elected independently.

Professionals—People who participate in the activities of political parties based on material or social incentives.

Proportional Representation—A method of selecting representatives in which representation is given to political parties based on the proportion of the vote obtained.

Recall—An election in which the voters decide whether to remove elected officials from office.

Referendum—The ability of the electorate to vote on proposed laws.

Responsible Party Model—A concept that describes democracies with strong competitive political parties, that win/retain office based on policy proposals, and enacts policies based electoral promises.

Single-Member-District-Plurality System—A method of selecting representatives in which one person will win the single position based on obtaining a plurality of the vote.

Split-Ticket Voting—Voting for candidates from more than one political party in a single election.

Third Parties—Minor political parties that periodically appear but have little success in winning office.

Two-Party System—A political system in which only two political parties have a realistic chance of controlling the major offices of government.

Application

1. Go on-line to the Republican National Committee and Democratic National Committee websites. Read the party platforms and in your own words compare what each party has to say on each of the following:

ISSUE	DEMOCRATIC PARTY	REPUBLICAN PARTY
The War in Iraq		
Abortion		
Health Care Reform		
Financial Aid for College Students		

2. In your own words, explain the factors which lead the U.S. to be a 2 party system.

3. In your own words, describe what is meant by the party in the electorate, the party organization, and the party in government.

4. Explain the meaning and significance of a critical election and an electoral realignment.

5. Identify and describe the characteristics that make the American party system distinctive.

6. Identify and describe the structure and functions of political parties.

7. Identify and describe the structure and functions of the national political party organizations. What is the nature of the relationship between the national parties and the state parties?

8. What is meant by the term minor party? Give an example of one.

9. Identify the minor parties which have been most successful and the conditions/factors of that time which enabled them to gain that success.

Multiple Choice Questions

1. The idea that political parties should be elected and retained based on their policy proposals is called:
    a. the responsible party model.
    b. the policy emphasis model.
    c. the policy preference model.
    d. none of the above.

2. The ability of a political party to require elected officials to carry out the party agenda is known as:
    a. party strength.
    b. party allegiance.
    c. party discipline.
    d. platform control.

3. The primary difference between political parties and interest groups is:
    a. the number of members.
    b. their objectives.
    c. the reasons people join.
    d. the methods used to influence politics.

4. The division of a political party which is made up of elected and appointed officeholders who are members of a party is known as:
    a. the party in government.
    b. the party in office.
    c. the party in the electorate.
    d. the party organization.

5. Which of the following is NOT one of the major divisions of political parties?
    a. the party in government
    b. the party in office
    c. the party in the electorate
    d. the party organization

6. Which of the following is NOT one of the functions of political parties?
    a. to provide accountability
    b. to motivate voters
    c. to simplify the choices for voters
    d. to manage societal conflict
    e. all of the above ARE functions of political parties

7. The party decline thesis is based upon the idea that:
   a. party organizations have little control over their candidates.
   b. party-line voting has decreased over time.
   c. party attachment among the people is weakening.
   d. all of the above.

8. Voting for candidates from more than one political party on a single ballot is known as:
   a. cross-over voting.
   b. split-ticket voting.
   c. ballot-breaking voting.
   d. party-splitting voting.

9. When one political party controls the White House and another controls Congress, it is called:
   a. gridlock.
   b. split-party control.
   c. divided control.
   d. divided government.

10. When a majority of Democrats in the legislature vote one way and a majority of the Republican votes another, it is called a:
    a. split-vote.
    b. partisan issue.
    c. party vote.
    d. all of the above.

11. The reforms which lead to the weakening of party organizations included:
    a. the use of the direct primary.
    b. reduction of the number of political patronage jobs.
    c. the use of non-partisan elections.
    d. all of the above.

12. An election which clearly reflects a new partisan alignment and produces a new partisan majority is known as a:
    a. realigning election.
    b. new party election.
    c. historical election.
    d. none of the above.

13. The incentives for associating with a political party include the attaining of:
    a. material benefits.
    b. social benefits.
    c. purposive benefits.
    d. all of the above.

14. When three of more political parties effectively compete for office and no single party dominates the process, it is called a:
    a. multiparty system.
    b. three-party system.
    c. true party system.
    d. responsible party system.

15. Which of the following is NOT one of the reasons the U.S. has traditionally had a two-party system?
    a. The U.S. has historically been divided into many factions and this developed into two parties.
    b. There is a good deal of consensus in the US about the goals of society and how to achieve them.
    c. The electoral rules of the U.S. favor the two parties.
    d. There is a natural perpetuation of the parties.

16. A political system which allocates seats in the legislature to parties based on the share of the vote they attain is known as a:
    a. presidential system.
    b. single-member-district system.
    c. proportional representation system.
    d. parliamentary system.

17. A political system which allocates seats in the legislature to parties based on who won the most votes in each district is known as:
    a. U.S. system.
    b. Single-member-district-plurality system.
    c. Winner-take-all system.
    d. Proportional representation system.

18. A political system which permits the party that controls the majority of seats in the legislature to select the chief executive is known as a:
    a. proportional system.
    b. presidential system.
    c. parliamentary system.
    d. executive system.

19. The power of the people to propose and enact legislation directly is known as:
    a. recall.
    b. referendum.
    c. direct democracy.
    d. initiative.

20. Minor parties in the U.S. have:
    a. influenced the number of Electoral College votes the two major party candidates for president have been able to attain.
    b. influenced the policy perspectives of the two major parties.
    c. been assimilated into the two major parties.
    d. all of the above.

Workbook Chapter 9 - Elections and Voting Behavior

Concepts

Allocation of National Party Convention Delegates

Apportionment

Campaign Finance

Determinants of Voter Choice

Determinants of Voting Participation

Effects of Voter Registration

Electoral College

Evolution of the Nomination Process

Financing Presidential Nomination Campaigns

Franchise

Incumbency Advantage

Models of Voting Behavior

Partisan Alignment of the Public

Process of Nominating Candidates for Congress

Process of Nominating Candidates for President

Reforming the Electoral College

Selection of Delegates

Voter Turnout

Key Terms

Advertising—The activities of members of Congress (such as sending out newsletters or visiting the district) designed to familiarize the constituency with the member.

Automatic Plan—A plan to prevent unfaithful Electoral College members that would automatically credit a candidate with a state's Electoral College votes upon winning the popular election and bypass the need for a formal vote of the Electoral College.

Blanket Primaries—A primary election in which all the parties are listed on a single ballot, enabling voters to participate in more than one political party.

Candidate Image—The people's perception of a candidate's qualities.

Caucus Method—A method by which state conventions select delegates to a political party's national convention.

Closed Primaries—A primary election open only to party members.

Credentials Committee—A committee at a political party's national convention that is responsible for reviewing the credentials of all the delegates and resolves any disputes over the delegation.

Credit Claiming—Efforts by members of Congress to get their constituents to believe they are responsible for positive government actions.

Critical Election—The first election that clearly reflects a new partisan alignment that produces a new partisan majority.

Descriptive Representation—The view of representation that calls for the racial and ethnic makeup of Congress to reflect that of the nation.

Deviating Election—An election in which the minority party is able to overcome the long-standing partisan orientation of the public based on temporary or short-term forces.

Direct Popular Election—Election of office holders directly by the people.

Direct Primary—The selection of a political party's candidate for the general election by a vote of party members.

District Plan—A plan to revise the Electoral College that would distribute a state's Electoral College votes by giving one vote to the candidate who wins a plurality in each House district and two votes to the winner statewide.

Electoral College—The institution (whose members are elected by the people) that is responsible for selecting the President of the United States.

Favorite Sons—A term used to refer to popular state officeholders.

Franchise—The constitutional or statutory right to vote.

Franking Privilege—The ability of members of Congress to send mail to their constituents free of charge.

Frontloading—The tendency of states to move their primaries earlier in the season in order to gain more influence over the presidential selection process.

General-Ticket System—A system in which a state's electoral college votes are awarded to the statewide winner of the popular vote.

Gerrymandering—The drawing of district lines to help or hinder the electoral prospects of a specific political party or individual.

Hard Money—Campaign contributions made directly to candidates and regulated by law.

Invisible Primary—The period of time between the election of one president and the first contest to select the next president.

Justiciable Issue—An issue or topic over which the courts have jurisdiction or the power to make decisions.

Keynote Address—An important speech given at a political convention designed to relay the tone of the convention and motivate party members.

King Caucus—Another name for the legislative caucus.

Legislative Caucus—A method of selecting political party candidates in which party members in the state legislature select candidates for statewide office and party members in the House of Representatives to select a party's candidate for president and vice president.

Magic Number—The number of delegates needed at a political party's national convention to be nominated as the party's candidate for the presidency.

Maintaining Election—An election in which the traditional majority party maintains power based on the long-standing partisan orientation of the voters.

Majority-Minority Districts—Districts in which the majority of the population is composed of ethnic and/or racial minorities.

Malapportioned—The distribution of legislative seats that does not accurately reflect the distribution of the population.

Mid-Term Elections—Congressional and gubernatorial elections that occur in the middle of a presidential term.

Multimember District—A method of selecting representatives in which more than one person is chosen to represent a single constituency.

National Party Convention—A meeting attended by delegates from each state to choose the party's candidates for president and vice president are chosen.

Nomination Process—The method used by political parties to select their candidates for the general election.

Nonpartisan Primary—A primary system used in Louisiana in which candidates from all political parties run in the same ballot and the candidate who receives the majority of the vote obtains the office.

One Person, One Vote—The principle established in the 1964 Supreme Court decision of *Wesberry v. Sanders*, that legislative districts must contain about the same number of people.

Open Primaries—A primary election that is open to independents and in some cases, member of other parties.

Open Seats—Elections in which there are no incumbents running for re-election.

Party Leaders—People who hold office within a political party.

Perquisites (Perks)—The benefits and support that members of Congress receive in order to help them perform their job.

Platform Committee—A committee at a political party's national convention that is responsible for drafting the document that states the beliefs and positions of the party.

Political Efficacy—The belief that participation in politics can make a difference.

Pork Barrel Benefits—Government-sponsored projects or expenditures that bring economic benefits to a member of Congress' district.

Position Taking—Making public statements on issues of importance to the constituency by members of Congress.

Proportional Plan—A plan to revise the Electoral College in which Electoral College votes are given to candidates based on the proportion of the popular vote they obtained.

Proportional Representation—A method of selecting representatives in which representation is given to political parties based on the proportion of the vote obtained.

Prospective Voting—Voting which is based on an individual's estimation of how well a candidate will perform duties in the future.

Rational Choice Model—A model of voter choice that suggests that voters first decide whether to vote and then base their candidate selection on rational calculation.

Realigning Election—An election in which the minority party wins by building a relatively stable coalition that endures over a series of elections.

Reapportionment—The process of adjusting the number of House seats among the states based on population shifts.

Redistricting—The process of redrawing district lines after House seats have been reapportioned.

Reinstating Election—An election in which the majority party regains power after a deviating election.

Retrospective Voting—Voting based on an individual's evaluation of the past performance of a candidate.

Rules Committee—A committee at a political party's national convention that is responsible for developing the rules governing conduct at the convention.

Run-off Primary—An election between the two candidates in a single political party who obtained the most votes in the primary in which no candidate received a majority, held to determine which will be the party's candidate in the general election.

Single-Member District—A method of selecting representatives in which the people in a district select a single representative.

Social-Psychological Model— An explanation of voter choice that focuses on individual attitudes.

Soft Money—Campaign contributions given to political parties rather than directly to candidates.

Sociological Model—An explanation of voter choice that considers such factors as religion, place of residence, and socioeconomic status.

State Presidential Primary—A method of selecting delegates to a political party's national convention in which the voters directly elect delegates.

Substantive Representation—The concept of representation, which states that officeholders do not have to be minorities to accurately represent minority, interests.

Superdelegates—Party leaders and elected officials chosen by state party officials and members of Congress, who attend the national convention as delegates uncommitted to any one candidate.

Swing States—States in which both presidential candidates have realistic chances of winning.

Unit Rule—A rule that requires the entire state delegation to a political party's national convention to vote the same way (or as a unit).

Voter Turnout—The percentage of eligible voters who cast votes in an election.

Application

1. Explain how the *timing* of primaries has influenced presidential campaigns.

2. Explain how the use of primaries to select candidates has influenced presidential campaigns.

3. In your own words, identify and explain the various criticisms of the Electoral College.

4. Explain the differences and similarities between the nomination processes for congressional and presidential candidates.

	Presidential Nominations	Congressional Nominations
Similarities		
Differences		

5. Identify and describe four proposals to reform the Electoral College and the problems they are designed to correct.

Plan	Description	Problem it is Designed to Correct

6. In your own words, identify the electoral advantages enjoyed by congressional incumbents.

7. In your own words, identify who votes and why.

8. Explain how funding can influence a Presidential candidate's success in the nomination process.

9. Explain the advantages and disadvantages of the following:

	Advantages	Disadvantages
Open primaries		
Closed primaries		
Blanket primaries		

10. In your own words explain how members of congress use their offices to appeal to constituents.

11. In your own words give examples of 5 different ways people can participate in politics.
1.

2.

3.

4.

5.

12. List five things you would recommend to increase voter turnout.
1.

2.

3.

4.

5.

13. Are you a retroactive or prospective voter? Explain why you would say that.

Multiple Choice Questions

1. An election to select a political party's candidate in which independents are welcome to vote is known as:
    a. closed primary
    b. open primary
    c. independent primary
    d. blanket primary

2. The most important determinant of the size of a state's delegation at the national party convention for both the Democratic and Republican parties is:
    a. state size
    b. the importance of the state to the party
    c. the state's economic importance
    d. how the state voted in the last presidential election

3. The functions of the national party convention include:
    a. conventions nominate candidates
    b. approve the party platform
    c. unify the party for the general election
    d. adopt the rules that govern the party
    e. all of the above

4. The patterns seen in the nomination of congressional candidates include:
    a. candidates get little or no help from the national party
    b. the sources of candidates are the same
    c. incumbents seldom loose
    d. all of the above

5. To be elected President, a candidate must receive:
    a. a plurality of the electoral votes, (more than any other candidate, not necessarily a majority)
    b. electoral votes from over 1/2 of the states
    c. a majority of the electoral votes
    d. a majority of the popular votes

6. If no candidate receives a majority of Electoral College votes then:
    a. the House of Representatives chooses the President from among the top three candidates with each state casting one vote
    b. the Senate chooses the President from among the top three candidates with each state casting one vote
    c. the President is elected by a majority of both Houses of Congress
    d. the candidate with the most votes (i.e. .a plurality) is elected

7. The number of electoral votes a state has is:
   a. determined by state legislatures
   b. determined by Congress
   c. determined by the formula in Article II of the Constitution
   d. equal to the number of representatives the state has in the U.S. Senate and the U.S. House of Representatives

8. The plan to reform the Electoral College which is designed to handle the problem of unfaithful electors and calls for a state's electoral college votes to simply be credited to the winner of the popular vote is known as the:
   a. proportional plan
   b. automatic plan
   c. district plan
   d. popular vote plan

9. The principal of "one person, one vote" as used by the Supreme Court in the reapportionment decisions means that:
   a. each voter may cast only one vote in an election
   b. each legislative district must contain approximately the same number of voters
   c. proxy voting where one person casts a vote for another person is permissible as long as both persons are qualified voters in the district
   d. all of the above have been included in the principle in different court cases

10. Which of the following statements correctly describes the success of incumbents in Congressional elections?
    a. incumbents in both the House and Senate are about equally likely to be reelected
    b. incumbents in the Senate are more likely to be reelected than incumbents in the House
    c. incumbents in the House are more likely to be reelected than incumbents in the Senate
    d. incumbency is not an advantage in Congressional elections

11. The view of representation which states that a member of Congress does not have to be of the same ethnic or racial background as his/her constituents to represent their interests is known as:
    a. real representation
    b. descriptive representation
    c. substantive representation
    d. none of the above

12. David Mayhew suggests that incumbents use their office to appeal to constituents through:
    a. position taking
    b. advertising
    c. credit claiming
    d. all of the above

13. Voter turnout in the U.S. is lower than in other western democracies because:
    a. the U.S. has more elections than other countries
    b. the U.S. has more cumbersome registration requirements than other nations
    c. the two-party system in the U.S. provides less choice for the voters than in other countries
    d. all of the above

14. The belief that participation in politics is important and can make a difference is known as:
    a. political efficacy
    b. participation confidence
    c. participation precedence
    d. none of the above

15. The influences on voter choice in Presidential elections include all of the following EXCEPT:
    a. issues
    b. candidate image
    c. money spent on ads
    d. party identification

16. Which of the following statements about party identification is true?
    a. People tend to change their party identification over the course of their lifetimes.
    b. Party identification is a strong predictor of voter choice.
    c. People often shift their party identification over the course of an election.
    d. All of the above are true statements.

17. All of the following conditions influence whether an issue will affect voter choice EXCEPT:
    a. voters must be aware of an issue
    b. voters must care about an issue
    c. voters must understand an issue
    d. voters must believe that one candidate would better represent their views on that issue than another

18. Voting based on the past performance of a candidate is known as:
    a. prospective voting
    b. achievement based voting
    c. past-based voting
    d. retrospective voting

19. An election which brings about major change and is based on the shift of long term partisan affiliation is known as:
    a. reinstating election
    b. installing election
    c. realigning election
    d. initiating election

20. The right to vote in the US has been extended in all of the following ways EXCEPT:
    a. the removal of lengthy residence requirements
    b. the elimination of the poll tax
    c. the removal of restrictions on ex-felons
    d. lowering of the voting age

Workbook Chapter 10 – Interest Groups

Concepts

Differences between Political Parties and Interest Groups

Free Rider Problem

Interest Group

Interest Group Activities

Interest Group Goals

Interest Group Power and Influence

Interest Group Resources

Interest Group Tactics

Material Benefits

Organizational entrepreneurship

Origin and Growth of Interest Groups

Power and Regulation of Interest Groups

Pressure Groups

Public Good

Purposive Benefits

Rationality and Interest Group Membership

Selective Benefits

Why People Join Interest Groups

Key Terms

Access (Political)—The ability to meet with and present one's ideas to political leaders.

Coalition Building—A means of expanding an interest group's influence that involves working with other groups.

Direct Lobbying—Direct contact by lobbyists with government officials in an effort to influence policy.

Free Rider—The problem of the rational person who chooses to enjoy the benefits of some group activity without incurring the costs.

Indirect Lobbying—The use of intermediaries by lobbyists to speak to government officials in their attempts to influence policy.

Interest Group—A group of people who come together based on shared beliefs or attitudes and attempt to influence government decision makers.

Lobbying—Activities in which a group or person attempt to influence public policymaking.

Lobbyists—Individuals who contact and attempt to influence governmental officials on behalf of others.

Logrolling—The exchange of support on issues between individuals or groups in order to gain mutual advantage.

Material Benefits—Tangible rewards gained from membership in an interest group.

Organization Entrepreneurs—People who seek the opportunity to create and build a group to satisfy underrepresented interests.

Political Action Committees (PACs)—Organizations created to raise money and make political contributions on behalf of an interest group.

Political Resources—The tools used by interests groups to influence the political process.

Pressure Group—A negative term used to describe an interest group.

Public Good—A benefit provided to everyone and cannot be withheld from those who did not participate in its provision.

Purposive Benefits—Interest group membership benefits that transcend the member's self-interest and are intended to improve society in general.

Rational—Pursuing individual self-interest by making decisions that maximize benefits and minimize costs.

Selective Benefits—Benefits provides by interest groups and isolated to members only.

Solidary Incentives—Intangible benefits gained from membership in an interest groups such as a sense of belonging to a group or meeting people with similar interests.

Tactics—The actions and ways interest groups use their political resources to influence the political process.

Application

1. In your own words, define what the free rider problem is and how interest groups seek to overcome this problem.

2. Find three different interest groups: One that appeals to members based on solidary benefits, one that appeals to members based on material benefits, and one that appeals to members based on purposive benefits. Write the name of the interest group (include the web address) and give an example of the type of benefit one might receive by joining.

Interest Group Name	Type of Benefit
1.	
2.	
3.	

3. Using one of the interest groups above (or a different one), identify three tactics used by the interest group to promote the agenda of the group. Briefly describe how the tactic promotes the agenda of the group.

Name of Interest Group: _____

Web Address of Interest Group:_____

Tactic	How the Tactic Promotes the Agenda of the Group
1.	
2.	
3.	

4. In your own words explain the difference between an interest group and a political party.

5. Identify 2 issues you care about. Do a web search to identify 2 interest groups which are related to these issues. Answer the following:

Issue	Interest Group and Web Address	Strategies used to Accomplish Group Goals

6. Imagine you were advising an interest group which deals with children's issues. Identify which parts of the legislative, executive and bureaucracy you would suggest the group work with to accomplish its goals.

Interest Group	Legislative Branch	Executive Branch	Bureaucracy

7. Identify the participants of an Iron Triangle.

    1.

    2.

    3.

8. Now select a policy area of interest to you (ex: the environment, health care, etc.).

Policy Area: _____

9. Now identify the specific participants in an Iron Triangle for this issue.

    1.

    2.

    3.

10. Name three factors which can influence the strength and power an interest group has to accomplish its policy goals.

    1.

    2.

    3.

Multiple Choice Questions

1. The differences between interest groups and political parties include:
   a. interest groups are private organizations while parties as public
   b. parties have a more general focus then do interest groups
   c. interest groups do not run candidates for office.
   d. All of the above

2. Interest group objectives include all of the following EXCEPT:
   a. to protect benefits from outside threats
   b. to promote the groups interests
   c. to prevent opposing groups success
   d. A, B, C all represent interest group objectives

3. Which of the following is NOT a reason people join interest groups?
   a. purposive benefits
   b. personal benefits
   c. material benefits
   d. solidary benefits

4. The benefits derived from interest group membership which is best described as attaining a sense of belonging and socializing with people who share ones interests is known as:
   a. purposive benefits
   b. personal benefits
   c. material benefits
   d. solidary benefits

5. A benefit that is given to everyone and cannot be withheld from those who did not contribute to its creation, is called a:
   a. public good
   b. private good
   c. material good
   d. none of the above

6. A benefit which is given only to interest group members and is given to attract members is called:
   a. purposive benefits
   b. selective benefits
   c. material benefits
   d. solidary benefits

7. Which of the following is an explanation for the formation of interest groups?
   a. As a response to social or economic events
   b. As a response to the expansion of the federal government
   c. As a response of the activities of organizational entrepreneurs.
   d. All of the above

8. Which of following is NOT a political resource of interest groups?
   a. money
   b. leadership
   c. connections
   d. membership

9. Which of the following is a tactic used by interest groups?
   a. coalition building
   b. shaping public opinion
   c. giving campaign support
   d. all of the above

10. When an interest group relays their views and concerns to political decision makers by using intermediaries, it is called:
    a. direct lobbying
    b. indirect lobbying
    c. intermediate lobbying
    d. none of the above

11. The idea that interest groups can act as a general stimulant for political participation is known as:
    a. unintentional mobilization
    b. unintentional participation
    c. unintentional voting
    d. unintentional activity

12. Organizations created specifically to raise money and contribute to political candidates are called:
    a. slush funds
    b. soft money groups
    c. interest groups
    d. party campaign organizations
    e. none of the above

13. Congress has restricted interest groups by all of the following EXCEPT:
    a. placing disclosure requirements on lobbyists
    b. limiting who can give contributions to candidates
    c. limiting the candidates to whom the groups may contribute
    d. limiting what interest groups may offer political candidates

14. A means of expanding an interest group's influence that involves working with other groups is known as:
    a. indirect lobbying
    b. organizational entrepreneurs
    c. coalition building
    d. rational tactics

15. The problem of interest groups not being able to exclude non-members from the benefits of group activities is known as the:
    a. free rider problem
    b. non-member problem
    c. no dues problem
    d. none of the above

16. People who see the opportunity to create and build an interest group are called:
    a. group entrepreneurs
    b. organizational framers
    c. organizational entrepreneurs
    d. group builders

17. Interest group membership benefits that are directed at non-members are known as:
    a. selective benefits
    b. public benefits
    c. solidary benefits
    d. purposive benefits

18. A negative term for interest groups, which describes the group as irresponsible and seeking benefits only for their own members, is _____.
    a. benefit group
    b. pressure group
    c. private interest group
    d. all of the above

19. Someone who is hired by an interest group to look after the groups interests in Washington is called a:
    a. hired gun
    b. direct lobbyist
    c. coalition builder
    d. professional lobbyist

20. When two or more interest groups agree to exchange support on different issues it is called:
    a. coalition building
    b. logrolling
    c. shared interests
    d. all of the above

Workbook Chapter 11 – Public Opinion

Concepts

Competence of Public Opinion

Elements of Public Opinion

Elites

Hyperdemocracy

Importance of Public Opinion in a Democracy

Interpreting Public Opinion Polls

Issue Publics

Issue Salience

Margin of Error

Origins of Public Opinion

Political Culture and how it Influences People's Beliefs

Political Socialization

Popular Sovereignty

Push Poll

Straw Poll

Key Terms

Agency Model of Representative Democracy—The idea that the job of elected leaders is to make decisions solely based on the views of the majority of the people.

Allegiant—The feeling of great trust and support for the political system.

Biased Sample—A sample (subset of a population) that does not accurately represent the population.

Civic Duty—The obligation felt by many to participate in politics.

Confidence Level—The degree to which there is assurance that the true results of a poll fall within the margin of error.

Direction—The idea of public opinion being either positive or negative (favorable or unfavorable) on an issue.

Efficacious—The belief that one's views are important and that government will listen and respond to them.

Elite Opinion—The attitudes or beliefs of people with a great deal of political influence.

Expressive Participation—The personal satisfaction gained from participating in politics.

Hyperdemocracy—The idea that policymakers have become so sensitive to public opinion that they are subservient to any brief shift in opinion.

Intensity—How strongly people hold the beliefs or attitudes that comprise public opinion.

Instrumental Participation—Participation in politics in order to accomplish a specific goal.

Instrumentation—The procedure of designing questionnaires.

Issue Public—A section of the public with a strong interest in a particular issue.

Margin of Error—The amount that sample responses are likely to differ from those of the actual population.

Political Alienation—The feeling of being isolated from or not part of the political process and system.

Political Culture—Shared ideas and beliefs of a culture concerning politics.

Political Participation—The translation of personal ideas and opinions into voluntary action designed to influence public policy.

Political Socialization—The process through which a younger generation learns political values from previous generations.

Popular Sovereignty—The idea that the highest political authority in a democracy is the will of the people.

Public Opinion—The sum of individual attitudes or beliefs about an issue.

Push Poll—A type of public opinion poll that intentionally uses leading or biased questions in order to manipulate the responses.

Random Sample—A method of selecting a sample (subset of the population) in which every person in the target population has an equal chance of being selected.

Reference Groups—Groups used by people as indicators for the appropriate views, opinions and behaviors.

Resource Model—An explanation of political participation that states that people need resources (time, money, and civic skills) in order to participate in politics.

Salience—The prominence or visibility of an issue or question.

Socioeconomic Status—The social background and economic position of a person.

Stability—The likelihood of changes in the direction of public opinion.

Straw Polls—Unscientific polls based on non-random samples.

Application

1. Identify and define the elements of public opinion.

Element	Definition

2. Identify and define the factors that influence political socialization.

Factor	Definition

3. Go to the Gallup Poll website (www.Gallup.com) and find the most recent information on the following issues:

Topic	Date of Poll	Question	Results
Immigration			
Cloning			
Economic Conditions			
Environment			
Terrorism			

4. If you were an elected official seeking to make policy which reflects the preferences of the American public, which of these policies would be the easiest to deal with? Why? Which of these would be the most difficult? Why?

5. Evaluate the following:

Percentage of Americans who favor changes in product labeling
            In Favor   26%
            Opposed   32%

What additional information would is necessary to evaluate the public opinion data presented above?

Multiple Choice Questions

1. The sum of individual attitudes or beliefs is known as:
    a. public opinion
    b. straw polls
    c. popular sovereignty
    d. none of the above

2. Which of the following are elements of public opinion?
    a. intensity
    b. stability
    c. salience
    d. direction
    e. all of the above

3. The prominence and visibility of an issue or question is referred to as _____.
    a. intensity
    b. stability
    c. salience
    d. direction

4. The idea that the job of elected leaders is make decisions solely based on the views of the majority of the people is known as _____
    a. popular sovereignty
    b. agency model of representation
    c. hyperdemocracy
    d. all of the above

5. A section of the public with intense interest in a particular issue is known as _____.
    a. elite public
    b. issue public
    c. interest group
    d. none of the above

6. Which of the following is NOT one of the questions used to evaluate public opinion polls?
    a. What was the question?
    b. What was the question ordering
    c. Who is the source of the poll?
    d. Did you ask the right people?

7. Unscientific polls which are based on non-random samples are known as _____
   a. straw polls
   b. paid polls
   c. public polls
   d. none of the above

8. A small subset of the population which is used ascertain the views or opinions of a larger group and does not accurately reflect the views of the population is known as a_____
   a. straw poll
   b. biased sample
   c. random sample
   d. haphazard sample

9. The amount of difference between the sample respondents and the actual population in a poll is called the _____.
   a. confidence level
   b. sampling error
   c. margin of error
   d. polling error

10. The process of designing survey questions is called _____.
   a. survey construction
   b. question construction
   c. instrument development
   d. instrumentation

11. The consensus or shared beliefs that bind a polity together are known as _____.
   a. political history
   b. shared opinion
   c. polity opinion
   d. political culture

12. Which of the following is NOT one of the agents of political socialization?
   a. schools
   b. media
   c. churches
   d. family

13. Which of the following is a form of political participation?
   a. sending a letter to a member of Congress
   b. contributing money to a candidate's campaign
   c. participating in a neighborhood project to clean up a local park
   d. all of the above

14. Which of the following would most likely yield the highest rates of participation?
    a. voting
    b. volunteering for a campaign
    c. contributing money to a campaign
    d. all of the above would yield about the same level of participation

15. The motivation for political participation that is based on the desire to accomplish a specific goal is known as _____.
    a. expressive participation
    b. efficacious participation
    c. instrumental participation
    d. none of the above

16. Feelings of isolation and estrangement from the political system are known as _____.
    a. allegiant feelings
    b. political isolation
    c. political efficacy
    d. political alienation

17. Which of the following is a determinant of political participation?
    a. psychological engagement in politics
    b. resources
    c. SES
    d. A person's social network
    e. All of the above

18. A person who expresses a great deal of trust in the political system is _____.
    a. allegiant
    b. alienated
    c. expressive
    d. none of the above

19. Which of the following are resources that effect political participation?
    a. money
    b. civic skills
    c. free time
    d. all of the above

20. Based on national trends, which of the following groups has the highest level of participation?
    - a. minorities
    - b. women
    - c. men
    - d. young people

Workbook Chapter 12 – Public Policy

<u>**Concepts**</u>

Agenda Setter

Agenda Setting

Arrow's Impossibility Theorem

Garbage Can Model

Incrementalism

Policy Evaluation

Policy Formulation and Adoption

Policy Implementation

Process vs. Impact Evaluation

Public Agenda

Stages of the Policy Making Process

<u>**Key Terms**</u>

Arrow's Impossibility Theorem—States that no decision making system can guarantee that the rank ordered preferences of a group will reflect the rank ordered preferences of the set of rational individuals who make up that group.

Feedback—The information policymakers receive through government reports, hearings, reading the news, casework, meetings with lobbyists and government officials, and contact with constituents.

Focusing Event—Event that grabs immediate attention and puts an issue on the public agenda.

Garbage Can Model—Theory which sought to explain why decisions in large organizations seems to be irrational.

Impact Evaluation—An evaluation undertaken to assess the outcomes or effects of a policy or program.

Incrementalism—A decision-making approach characterized by making current decisions that are small adjustments to past decisions.

Independent Regulatory Agency—A bureaucratic agency that sets and enforces standards for specific industries. Independent regulatory agencies have executive, legislative, and judicial authority and are designed to be outside the political control of any president or members of Congress.

Indicators—Any measures that can be employed as systematic monitoring devices.

Institutional Agenda—A short list of items being given serious consideration by policymaking institutions.

Policy Evaluation—The examination of the consequences of public policy.

Policy Formation and Adoption—Developing and choosing a course of action in response to a policy problem or issue.

Policy Implementation—Translating government intent into government action.

Process Evaluation—An evaluation undertaken with the goal of assessing whether a program or policy is being implemented according to its stated guidelines.

Public Agenda—All issues and problems that have the attention of the government at a particular point in time.

Public Policy—A course of action pursued by government officials or agencies.

Rational-Comprehensive Decision Making—A decision-making approach characterized by consideration of all alternatives to a problem or issue, an analysis of the costs and benefits of each alternative, and selection of the alternative with the most benefits at the least cost.

Application

1. Go on line to the website of an independent regulatory agency and list and describe an executive, a legislative, and a judicial function.

   Name of Agency: _____

   Web Address of the
   Agency: _____

Function	Description
1. Legislative	
2. Executive	
3. Judicial	

2. Go to the Federal Reserve web page http://www.federalreserve.gov, choose two policy tools, list them and in your own words, briefly describe them.

Policy Tool	Description

3. In your own words, explain the stages of policymaking. Give an example of each.

4. By reading or watching a current news source or going to www.whitehouse.gov, choose two issues on the public agenda, list them, and identify the government's response to those agenda items.

Agenda Item	Government Response
1.	
2.	

5. Go to http://dtvfacts.com, identify and in your own words describe the purpose of the DTV converter box and the role of government subsidies in the DTV converter box initiative.

Multiple Choice Questions

1. Stages in the policy-making process include all of the following EXCEPT:
    a. issue identification.
    b. policy formulation.
    c. policy communication.
    d. agenda setting.

2. Public policy is:
    a. Goal oriented.
    b. Undertaken by governments.
    c. A relatively stable course of action.
    d. All of the above.

3. Policy conflicts over symbolic issues are often the most difficult to resolve because:
    a. They involved fundamental beliefs about what is right and wrong.
    b. Compromise is less likely than on questions of tangible benefits.
    c. Compromise is unlikely to make any of the parties happy.
    d. All of the above.

4. The stage in the policymaking process which entails the consideration of alternative solutions is known as:
    a. Policy formulation.
    b. Policy selection.
    c. Policy evaluation.
    d. Policy alteration.

5. The list of issues and problems on which government focuses is known as:
    a. the policy agenda.
    b. the national agenda.
    c. the public agenda.
    d. the policy goals.

6. Which of the following groups would NOT be considered agenda setters?
    a. Interest groups
    b. The courts
    c. The states
    d. Congress

7. The garbage can model of agenda setting suggests:
    a. That possible solutions are often developed without a specific problem to be solved.
    b. That policy makers can find solutions to problems by looking at pre-determined possible policy responses.
    c. That problems and solutions are seen as the product of independent processes.
    d. All of the above.

8. When policy questions rise to predominance after a crisis or emergency, those are knows as:
    a. Focusing events.
    b. Crisis management policies.
    c. Emergency management policy development.
    d. Non-routine policy indicators.

9. The short list of policy items on which action can be taken policy makers give serious consideration, are known as:
    a. The real policy agenda.
    b. The institutional agenda.
    c. The President's agenda.
    d. The "short list".

10. Which of the following statements about rational-comprehensive decision making in policy is accurate?
    a. It assumes that policy formation and adoption considers all options.
    b. It is not very practical.
    c. It assumes that policymakers have complete information.
    d. All of the above statements are accurate.

11. The method of developing policy which starts by looking at how similar problems have been dealt with in the past and then identifies solutions which are feasible is known as:
    a. Realistic policy making.
    b. Incrementalism.
    c. Historical development of policy.
    d. All of the above.

12. Policy evaluation is conducted for all of the following reasons EXCEPT:
    a. To see if the policy was properly implemented.
    b. To see if the policy is serving the needs of the recipients.
    c. To see if the policy is in compliance with bureaucratic standards.
    d. To see if the policy achieved its goals efficiently and effectively.

13. Ken Mayer points out that some public policies fail because:
    a. They regulate behavior which is not really problematic.
    b. They have not been properly designed.
    c. The public wants them to fail.
    d. They are outdated and no longer apply to current conditions.

14. Which of the following statements about policymaking and the core democratic principle of majority rule are accurate?
    a. U.S. policymaking has traditionally done a good job protecting minority rights.
    b. U.S. policymaking has traditionally done a good job representing the views of the majority.
    c. People are generally happy with the policies made in the U.S.
    d. All of the above.

15. The core democratic principle of Political Freedom is evident in the policy making process by:
    a. People being free to express their views about the need for new policy.
    b. People being able to give input on the evaluation of policy.
    c. People being able to protest policies with which they disagree.
    d. All of the above.

16. Political equality is the core democratic principle which is most difficult to achieve in policy making because:
    a. Not all people have equal access to the policymaking process.
    b. Not all people have equal access to the policy makers.
    c. Not everyone has the money or resources to participate in policymaking.
    d. All of the above.

17. Arguments in favor of incrementalism in policymaking include:
    a. It provides a justification for each new development in policy.
    b. Policymakers do not always have time or money to consider all possible options, so the use of a baseline policy is useful.
    c. It is predictable.
    d. All of the above.

18. Policy evaluation which assesses policy outcomes is known as:
    a. Outcome based evaluation.
    b. Process evaluation.
    c. Impact evaluation.
    d. Success indicator evaluation.

19. The policy implications of Arrow's Impossibility Theorem include:
    a. The idea that there is no way to be certain what policies people actual want or prefer.
    b. The idea that there is no decision making system which can guarantee that ranking of preference of the group will represent those of the people.
    c. Whoever sets the agenda can influence group decisions.
    d. All of the above.

20. Which of the following is NOT used in selecting issues for the public agenda?
    a. Feedback information
    b. Legislative interest
    c. Indicators
    d. Focusing events